Watfo Palace

present

G000167123

Poppy
+George

by Diane Samuels

Poppy + George was first performed at
Watford Palace Theatre on 12 February 2016

Poppy +George

by Diane Samuels

Cast (in alphabetical order)
Nadia Clifford
Jacob Krichefski
Rebecca Oldfield
Mark Rice-Oxley

Creative Team

Director	Jennie Darnell
Designer	Ruari Murchinson
Composer/Sound Designer	Gwyneth Herbert
Lighting Designer	David Holmes
Voice and Dialect Coach	Penny Dyer
Movement Director	Scarlett Mackmin
Assistant Director	Lucy Barrett
Company Stage Manager	Maddie Baylis
Deputy Stage Manager	Emma Hansford
Assistant Stage Manager	Emma Ryan
Wardrobe Supervisor	Mark Jones
Costume Makers	Michelle Bristow
	Sarah Ninot
Hair and Make-up Adviser	Clare Parker

Author's Note

Poppy + George has a past life with another name.

In the early 1990s, as Writer-in-Residence at Theatre Centre, a young people's theatre company, I was researching into the lives, loves and misdeeds of women pirates of the eighteenth century when I stumbled upon various other intrepid women who lived outside the 'feminine' remit. I loved their independence of spirit. From the perspective of the end of the twentieth century, I found myself wanting to step into a moment in time when the opportunities (education, health resources and legal rights, etc.) from which I benefited, due in some way to these women of former eras, began to take effect for women in general. Looking back to where the century began I was drawn to the year after the Great War ended, 1919. Change was in the air. All the known boundaries and definitions of class, nationhood, gender roles that had been in place before the war were shifting in essential ways for men as well as women. Clothes were changing too. And clothes say and do so much. In my imagination, a tailor and dressmaker's workshop, tucked away down passages and alleyways, hidden from many, took shape. Here, whilst the world outside was in flux, identities were being crafted and many different worlds created by the cut of a jacket, the flare of a skirt or the line of a pair of trousers. As Oscar Wilde wrote, 'It is only shallow people who do not judge by appearances. The true mystery of the world is the visible, not the invisible...' I wanted to explore the mystery of the visible. And so they sprung to life – Smith the Chinese tailor; George the chauffeur; Tommy Johns the music-hall female-impersonator back from a tour of duty in the trenches; and a young woman from the north of England, inspired by her Suffragette teacher, named Melody. *Turncoat*, as the play was then called, ventured on tour throughout the UK not long after a law introduced under Mrs Thatcher's government a few years earlier had made the promotion of homosexuality in schools illegal.

Twenty years later, nearly a century after the play is set, in the second decade of the twenty-first century, it has emerged from the filing cabinet with a whoosh. Watford's Palace Theatre, once a music hall at the beginning of the twentieth century, is the perfect venue – a renovated building with a history that rings to the songs in the play. Same-sex couples marry, men wear dresses, women wear beards, many other women wear the veil – definitions of gender are shifting, veering from one extreme to the other, questions and certainty vie in volatile contrast. Who am I? Who are we? These questions are stronger than ever. A new time, a new place, and so a new name. *Poppy + George* popped into my mind without bidding. I felt moved to rename the young woman at the heart of the play, Poppy. I didn't quite know why at first, despite the obvious connections with the commemorative flower for those fallen in war – although that wasn't introduced until 1921. But as I immersed myself in rewriting, Poppy began to grow into her name and the play into its new title in unexpected ways. The potent symbolism of this flower has now infused the work – dreams, ending, roots, transformation, resurrection – and the way the seeds sleep silently in the earth until the soil is disrupted (often by war as much as farming or trampling of boots or hooves) and then the latent potential is released. Somehow this is a theme for these times too – a call to notice, to look again, to see how disruption and change, scary, shattering and unnerving though they may be, can enable hidden seeds of untapped flowering within each individual as well as the collective to stir into life, rise up and blossom at last.

Diane Samuels
January 2016

Cast Biographies

NADIA CLIFFORD
Nadia trained at Bristol Old Vic Theatre School.

Theatre includes: *Pomona* (National Theatre/Orange Tree); *Hobson's Choice* (Regent's Park); *PIIGS* (Royal Court); *Clean* (Traverse); *Old Money* (Hampstead); *The Breakout* (Young Vic); *Twelfth Night* (Drayton); *Through the Night* (Finborough); *Coasting* (Bristol Old Vic); *Country Music* (Trafalgar Studios).

JACOB KRICHEFSKI
Jacob trained at Webber Douglas.

Theatre includes: *The Great Extension* (Theatre Royal Stratford East); *Blue Sky* (Pentabus/Hampstead); *The Seagull, The Hamlet Project* (The Factory); *The Tempest* (York Theatre Royal/Sprite); *Lucifer Saved* (Finborough); *2000 YRS, Market Boy* (National Theatre).

Television includes: *The Casual Vacancy, Holby City, Silent Witness, Casualty, Maisie Raine, Preston Front* (BBC); *Borgia* (Canal+); *The Honourable Woman* (BBC Worldwide); *A Touch of Frost* (Yorkshire Television); *The Bill* (ITV); *Sex Traffic* (CH4); *Family Affairs* (CH5); *Iechyd Da* (S4C).

Film includes: *Suffragette* (Ruby Films/Pathé/Film4).

Radio includes: *The Kiss – The Advertiser* (BBC Radio 4).

REBECCA OLDFIELD
Rebecca trained at Webber Douglas.

Theatre includes: *Worst Wedding Ever* (Salisbury Playhouse); *The Love Girl and the Innocent, Faith, Hope and Charity* (Southwark Playhouse); *A Midsummer Night's Dream* (Regent's Park); *Taken, That Almost Un-nameable Lust* (Soho/Clean Break), *Labour Day* (Bush); *Is Everyone Ok?* (Nabokov regional tour).

Television includes: *Silent Witness, Doctor Who, Holby City, Afterlife, The Silence, Doctors, Knifeman* (Pilot).

Film includes: *Ghecko, Powder Room, The Edge of Tomorrow.*

MARK RICE-OXLEY
Mark trained at Webber Douglas.

Theatre includes: *Bright Phoenix, The Kindness of Strangers* (Liverpool Everyman); *Playing With Grown Ups* (Brits Off Broadway); *Afraid of the Dark* (Charing Cross); *Tanzi Libre* (Southwark Playhouse); *Blood Brothers* (Phoenix); *Town* (Royal & Derngate); *Switzerland* (HighTide Festival); *Much Ado About Nothing, The Merchant of Venice, Holding Fire* (Shakespeare's Globe); *Pool (No Water)* (Frantic Assembly); *The Romans in Britain* (Crucible Sheffield); *The Life of Galileo* (Birmingham Rep); *David Copperfield* (West Yorkshire Playhouse);*The Entertainer* (Liverpool Playhouse); *The Comedy of Errors* (Bristol Old Vic); *Cuckoos* (Barbican); *The Dwarfs* (Tricycle); *Workers Writes* (Royal Court); *The Danny Crowe Show* (Bush); *Cressida* (Albery).

Television includes: *Whitechapel, WPC 56, Doctors, Preston Passion, Land Girls, New Tricks, Hotel Babylon, EastEnders, Holby City, The Dwarfs, Mersey Beat, Judge John Deed, In Deep, Two Pints of Lager and a Packet of Crisps.*

Film includes: *In His Life: The John Lennon Story* (as George Harrison).

DIANE SAMUELS (Writer)

Diane Samuels was born and raised in Liverpool. She currently lives in London where she has been working as a playwright and author since the early 1990s. She enjoys collaborating across art forms, with composers, musicians, visual artists, dance specialists, and draws on relationships with scientists, historians, psychotherapists, medical practitioners, healers to expand the scope of her practice and work. She also works as a teacher/facilitator of creative writing to all ages.

Kindertransport won the Verity Bargate and Meyer-Whitworth Awards, and was first produced by Soho Theatre Company in 1993. It has been translated into many languages, performed in the West End, Off Broadway and all over the world, revived in 2007 in the UK by Shared Experience Theatre Company. Now studied for A and A/S Level and a set text for English Literature GCSE. Other plays include *The True-Life Fiction of Mata Hari*, Watford Palace Theatre, 2002; *Cinderella's Daughter*, Trestle Theatre tour, 2005; and *3 Sisters on Hope Street* (with actress Tracy-Ann Oberman), after Chekhov, co-produced by Liverpool Everyman/Playhouse and Hampstead Theatres, 2008. *The Arrest of Rosa Gold*, readings at National Theatre Studio, 2010, and Jewish Museum, 2012. *End of Romance*, performed reading as part of the Mary Shelley Festival, Bournemouth, 2011.

For younger audiences, plays include *One Hundred Million Footsteps* for Quicksilver Theatre Company; *Chalk Circle*, *Frankie's Monster* and *How to Beat a Giant* at the Unicorn Theatre.

For BBC radio, plays include *Swine*, *Doctor Y*, *Watch Out for Mister Stork*, *Hen Party*, *Tiger Wings*, five part serial for Woman's Hour, and *Psyche*.

She has wide experience of teaching creative writing, lecturing at the universities of Birmingham, Reading, Oxford, Goldsmiths' and running workshops for Institute for Arts in Therapy and Education, Alternatives, Theatre Royal Haymarket and the National Gallery. She was Royal Literary Fund Fellow at the University of Westminster, 2008 to 2011, and has been visiting lecturer at Regent's College, London, from 2013. She runs a regular writers' group and is writer-in-residence at Grafton Primary School, Islington, North London.

Diane was one of a creative team awarded a Science on Stage and Screen Award by the Wellcome Trust in 2001 leading to *PUSH*, The People Show Studios, 2003. Her short story, *Rope*, broadcast as one of the 2002 winners of BBC Radio 4's online short story competition. Writer and presenter *Inter-Rail Postcards*, BBC Radio 3. Interactive writing installation, *In Your Own Words* for Battersea Arts Centre's One on One Festival, 2011. As Pearson Creative Research Fellow 2004/5 at the British Library, completed research into magic, booklet *A Writer's Magic Notebook*, pub. 2006.

Recently, Diane has written *Persephone (A Love Story)*, with composer Maurice Chernick, Arts Council England funding for staged readings at Rosemary Branch theatre, 2013; and *The A-Z of Mrs P*, music/lyrics by Gwyneth Herbert, world premiere Southwark Playhouse, 2014.

Diane is also writing, with Maurice Chernick, a new oratorio with spoken word, *Song of Dina* that gives voice to the invisibled daughter of biblical patriarch Jacob to be given a public presentation of work in progress at JW3 in April 2016.

Also, in development are: *The Rhythm Method* with Gwyneth Herbert, probing the ins and outs of contraception, recipient of a Wellcome Trust award; and *A Waltz & a Prayer* exploring marriage, faith, miracles and the possible sainthood of Mother Cornelia Connelly.

JENNIE DARNELL (Director)
Jennie directed *Brighton Beach Memoirs* for Watford Palace Theatre.

She has been an Associate Director for Plymouth Theatre Royal for whom she directed: *Merit, Blood Red Saffron Yellow, Musik, The Imposter, Union Street, True West, All My Sons, Burn This* and *The Woman Who Cooked Her Husband*. She was also an Associate Director for Hampstead Theatre where she directed *The Dead Eye Boy,* and *U.S & Them.*

Other theatre credits include: *The New Statesman* (Trafalgar Studio's/No 1 tour); *On the Ceiling* (Birmingham Rep); *Clouds* (No 1 tour); *One Under* (Tricycle);

Further credits include: *Office Suite* and *The Messiah* (West Yorkshire Playhouse); *Rumpelstiltskin, Pandora, Telling Tales* and *The Woman Who Cooked Her Husband* (Nottingham Playhouse); *Lady Windermere's Fan* (Salisbury Playhouse); *Up on the Roof* (Mercury, Colchester); *Wallflowering* (national tour); *'Tis Pity She's a Whore* (Derby Playhouse); *Life x 3* (West End/tour). She was an Associate Director on *Art* (West End).

Television directing includes: *EastEnders* (director of BAFTA and RTS award-winning episodes), *Holby City* and *Doctors.*

RUARI MURCHISON (Designer)
Design credits include: *Mappa Mundi, Frozen, The Waiting Room, The Red Balloon* (National Theatre); *Titus Andronicus* (Royal Shakespeare Company); *Othello* [Trafalgar Studios]; *The Solid Gold Cadillac* (Garrick); *A Busy Day* (Lyric); *Peggy Sue Got Married* (Shaftesbury); *The Snowman* (Peacock) *Toyer, Betty and Jane* (Arts); *Three Sisters on Hope Street, The Glass Room, Gone to L.A.* (Hampstead); *Henry IV Parts I and II* (Washington Shakespeare Company, USA); *West Side Story, The Sound of Music* (Stratford Festival, Canada); *Hamlet* (Elisnore, Denmark); *Oleanna, Educating Rita, Pravda, The Critic, The Real Inspector Hound* (Chichester).

Ruari has designed for almost all the regional theatres in the United Kingdom including Birmingham Rep [Associate Artist], West Yorkshire Playhouse, Northern Stage, Watford Palace, Bristol Old Vic, Nottingham Playhouse, Plymouth Theatre Royal, Liverpool Everyman and Playhouse, Derby Playhouse, Salisbury Playhouse, Theatr Clwyd.

Opera credits include: *Der Freischutz* (Finnish National Opera); *Peter Grimes, Così fan Tutte* (Luzerner Opera); *La Cenerentola, Il Barbiere di Siviglia* (Garsington); *L'Italiana in Algeri* (Buxton); *Les Pelerins de la Mecque, ZaZa* (Wexford).

Ballet credits include: *Bruise Blood* (Shobana Jeyasingh Dance Company); *Landschaft und Erinnerung* (Stuttgart Ballet, Germany); *The Protecting Veil* (Birmingham Royal Ballet); *The Snowman* (Seoul, London, Birmingham Rep/tour).

Ruari has taught technical students at LAMDA, Bristol Old Vic Theatre School, Central School of Speech and Drama and RADA where he has also worked on the MA Directors course. He has teaches student theatre designers in costume and set design at Nottingham Trent University.

GWYNETH HERBERT (Composer/Sound Designer)
Gwyneth Herbert is an award-winning composer, lyricist and multi-instrumentalist.

Theatre credits include: two collaborations with Diane Samuels – *The A–Z of Mrs P* (Southwark Playhouse) and *The Rhythm Method* (in development, Watford Palace Theatre, supported by The Wellcome Foundation); two one-act musical adaptations with bookwriter Christine Denniston – of Terrence Rattigan's *After Lydia* (winner of Sounds of England commission, staged reading at Watermill Theatre, Newbury, dir. Maria Freidman) and Peter Barnes' *Before the Law* (Sidney Brown Award Special Commendation, staged reading at Drury Lane, dir. Matthew Ryan); and *Le Tabou* with Kath Burlinson (YMT, Plymouth Barbican). With artist Mel Brimfield she's created two musical/art/film installations: *The Palace That Joan Built* – an Art on the Underground/Theatre Royal Stratford East commission celebrating the work of theatrical revolutionary Joan Littlewood, and *Springtime for Henry (and Barbara):* a multi-phase project exploring the life and works of sculptors Henry Moore and Barbara Hepworth (many venues including Wilton's Music Hall).

She has also released six albums under her own name (including *The Sea Cabinet,* developed with Aldeburgh Music, which enjoyed a UK-wide theatre tour); conducted her own film score at the BFI; staged a multi-lingual show in Mombasa, Kenya; composed for the London Sinfonietta; presented for BBC Radio 3 and 4; and had her arrangement of a Swahili folk song performed by 100,000 children around the world at once.

DAVID HOLMES (Lighting Designer)

David trained at the Theatre Royal; Glasgow and the Guildhall School of Music and Drama.

Theatre includes: *Abigail's Party & Shiv* (Curve); *Backbeat* (Duke of York's, London/ Los Angeles/Toronto); *James and the Giant Peach, Beryl* (West Yorkshire Playhouse); *Hotel* (National Theatre); *Cat on a Hot Tin Roof* (Novello); *King John, The Gods Weep, Days of Significance* (RSC); *An Intervention* (Paines Plough); *The Nutcracker* (Nuffield, Southampton); *Kasimir & Karoline, Fanny & Alexander* (Malmo Stadsteater Sweden); *Hello/Goodbye* (Hampstead); *Donny's Brain, Belongings* (Hampstead Downstairs/Trafalgar Studios); *Benefactors* (Sheffield); *A Midsummer Night's Dream* (Headlong/UK tour); Wagner Charity Gala in honour of His Royal Highness The Prince of Wales' 65th Birthday at Buckingham Palace, Wagner 200th Anniversary Concert, Berlioz's *Romeo and Juliet, Bluebeard's Castle* (also European Tour & San Francisco Symphony); *Gurrelieder, Peer Gynt, Il prigioniero* (for the Philharmonia Orchestra at the Royal Festival Hall); *Journey's End, Moonlight and Magnolias, The Rise and Fall of Little Voice, Rope* (Watermill, Newbury); *Remembrance Day, Alaska* (Royal Court); *Rusalka* (ETO); *Goalmouth* (The Sage, Gateshead); *Ma Vie En Rose, Creditors* (Young Vic); *Cannibals, Widowers' Houses, A Taste of Honey, See How They Run, Pretend You Have Big Buildings, Cyrano de Bergerac, Harvey and Roots* (Royal Exchange Theatre, Manchester); *Sweetness and Badness* (WNO); *After Miss Julie, Othello, Woman in Mind, Be My Baby* (Salisbury Playhouse); *Stallerhof, The Trestle at Pope Lick Creek* (Southwark Playhouse); *Fijis and Inside* (Jean Abreu Dance); *The Fantasticks, Ain't Misbehavin', House and Garden, Cleo, Camping, Emmanuelle and Dick* (Harrogate).

PENNY DYER (Voice and Dialect Coach)

Penny has been a leading specialist in her field for over thirty years.

Recent theatre includes: *The End of Longing* (West End); *Husbands and Sons* (RNT); *Teddy Ferrara* (Donmar Warehouse); *Gypsy* (Savoy/CFT); *The Maids; The Ruling Class* (Trafalgar Studios); *Assassins* (Chocolate Factory); *Linda, The Wolf from the Door, The Mistress Contract, Circle Mirror Transformation* (Royal Court); The Michael Grandage Company Season; *Good People, 55 Days* (Hampstead); *Other Desert Cities, Sweet Bird of Youth, Speed the Plow* (Old Vic); *This House, Blood and Gifts* (RNT); *The Promise, Roots* (Donmar Warehouse); *Posh, Clybourne Park* (Royal Court/Duke of York's); *The Commitments* (Palace); *The Book of Mormon* (Duke of York's); *Kiss Me Kate, The Resistible Rise of Arturo Ui* (WE/CFT).

Television includes: *The Rack Pack, The Last Kingdom, Code of a Killer, Marvellous, The Missing, Tubby and Enid, Cilla, Tommy Cooper, The Girl, Mrs Biggs, The Café, The Slap, Downton Abbey, Gracie, Small Island, Margaret, Most Sincerely, Fantabuloso, Blackpool, The Deal.*

Film includes: *The Danish Girl, Dad's Army, Florence Foster Jenkins, A Street Cat Named Bob, The Jungle Book, Pride, Testament of Youth, Blue Jasmine, Philomena,*

Sunshine on Leith, Kill Your Darlings, Tamara Drewe, Nowhere Boy, The Damned United, The Queen, Frost/Nixon, Mrs Henderson Presents, Infamous, Dirty Pretty Things, The War Zone, Elizabeth.

SCARLETT MACKMIN (Movement Director)

Scarlett Mackmin's previous productions include: *The Silver Tassie, Liolá, Welcome to Thebes, London Assurance, Really Old, Like 45, England People Very Nice, Burnt by the Sun, The President of an Empty Room* (National Theatre); *Di and Viv and Rose, Speaking in Tongues, Arcadia, Under the Blue Sky, In Celebration* (West End); *Private Lives* (West End/Theatre Royal Bath/Toronto/New York); *Dancing at Lughnasa* (Old Vic); *The Dark Earth and the Light Sky, Cloud Nine, Dying For It, The Hypochondriac, ID* (Almeida); *Privates on Parade* (Olivier Award nomination), *Caligula, After Miss Julie, The Dark* (Donmar Warehouse); *Sleeping Beauty* (Young Vic/Barbican/New York); *Peribanez* (Young Vic); *The Chairs* (Gate, Notting Hill); *The Merry Wives of Windsor* (RSC/also Old Vic/Michigan and tour); *A Midsummer Night's Dream, Two Gentlemen of Verona* (Regent's Park); *Up on the Roof* (Chichester); *A Doll's House* (Birmingham Rep/tour); *In Flame* (Bush/West End); *Air swimming* (tour); *The Tempest* (Sheffield Crucible/Old Vic); *A Midsummer Night's Dream, Cloud Nine, Iphigenia, The Arbor, Bird Calls* (Sheffield Crucible).

Film includes: *A United Kingdom, The Imitation Game, Pride and Prejudice and Zombies, Cemetery Junction, The King's Speech, Stage Beauty, Chocolat, The Last Minute* and *Miss Julie.*

Television includes: *Taboo, The Crown, Dancing on the Edge, Hattie* and *A Touch of Frost.*

Opera includes *Don Carlo* at the Royal Opera House.

LUCY BARRETT (Assistant Director)

Lucy Barrett is currently an MA Directing student at East 15 Acting School where she has been under the guidance of Matthew Lloyd, James MacDonald, Bijan Sheibani, Che Walker and Lucy Kirkwood. Previous to commencing her studying here, Lucy was a graduate of both Arts Educational, Chiswick in Musical Theatre and the University of Lincoln in Theatre (Awarded Student of the graduating year). After graduating from Lincoln, Lucy worked for the Lincoln Performing Arts Centre and The Lincoln Company, directing and assisting on shows such as *The Lion, The Witch and the Wardrobe* (LPAC, 2013), *The History Boys* (LPAC, Louth Riverhead 2014), *Abigail's Party* (LPAC, Louth Riverhead, South Holland Centre Spalding, Trinity Arts Centre Gainsborough 2014), *The Cosmonaut's Last Message to the Woman he Once Loved in the Former Soviet Union* (LPAC, Edinburgh Fringe 2014) and *Alice in Winter Wonderland* (LPAC, 2014). Since moving to London in September, Lucy has assisted two plays written and directed by Whit Hertford, *Dirtybird* and *Dottir,* as well as directing *The Beasts* in early January, a play written by Shane Humberstone and inspired by Shakespeares' Benedick and Beatrice in *Much Ado About Nothing* (The Courtyard, Hoxton).

THANKS

Thanks to Michael Musillo and Pino from Ego Hair Design, everyone at Cosprop, and Alan Dein for his recording of Yiddish Eastenders from his Radio 4 programme *Lives in a Landscape.*

Poppy + George in rehearsal

Jacob Krichefski

Nadia Clifford

Mark Rice-Oxley

Jacob Krichefski

Mark Rice-Oxley

Nadia Clifford and Mark Rice-Oxley

Richard Lakos Photography

**Watford
Palace Theatre**

Is a twenty-first-century producing theatre, making new work across the art forms of theatre, dance, outdoor arts and digital, and developing audiences, artists and communities through exciting opportunities to participate.

Watford Palace Theatre commissions and produces plays from a range of new and established writers. Recent premieres include *Coming Up* by Neil D'Souza; *Jefferson's Garden* by Timberlake Wertenbaker; *Love Me Do* by Laurence Marks and Maurice Gran; *An Intervention* by Mike Bartlett (in a co-production with Paines Plough); *Shiver* by Daniel Kanaber; the *Ideal World* season of three new plays – *Perfect Match* by Gary Owen, *Virgin* by E.V. Crowe (in a co-production with nabokov), *Override* by Stacey Gregg; *Jumpers for Goalposts* by Tom Wells (in co-production with Paines Plough and Hull Truck Theatre); *Our Brother David* by Anthony Clark; *Our Father* by Charlotte Keatley; and *Family Business* by Julian Mitchell.

Creative Associates are central to Watford Palace Theatre's vision these include resident companies **Rifco Arts** and **Tiata Fahodzi**; **Mahogany Opera Group**; **Scamp Theatre**; **Kate Flatt**; **Shona Morris**; **Charlotte Keatley**; **Gary Owen**; **Alice Birch** and **Timberlake Wertenbaker**.

Coming Up

An Intervention

Jefferson's Garden

Shiver

Love Me Do

Jumpers for Goalposts

www.watfordpalacetheatre.co.uk

Friends

Support a local theatre with a national reputation

Our Friends receive (£45 per annum)

Priority information and Booking
Discounted tickets (up to 20% on most performances)
20% discount on all beverages in our Cafe & Bar
No card payment, postage or exchange fees

Our Good Friends receive (£90 per annum)

All of the above plus:
10% discount on hires of WPT Green Room Bar, Cafe & Hospitality Room
Private backstage tours for up to 6 guests (normally £20)
Acknowledgement in show programmes for WPT productions

Our Best & Business Friends receive (£500+ per annum)

Private backstage tours for up to 12 guests (normally £30)
Complimentary press night tickets plus drinks
Opportunities to meet the cast of selected productions
And more exclusive offers

With thanks to the Friends of Watford Palace Theatre for their generous donations:

Business Friends

Metro Printing
Warner Bros. Studios, Leavesden
Bushey Hall Garage

Best Friends

Bev and Paul Jullien and family
Deborah Lincoln
Frank and Helen Neale
Graham and Claire Buckland

Good Friends

Peter Freuchen
Paul Harris
Jarmo Kesanto
Steve and Lois Magraw
Chris & Mary Mitchell
Frank and Helen Neale
M Parker
Linda Patel
Gary Townsend-Vila and David Dominguez-Vila
Norman and Mavis Tyrwhitt
PGC Young

Help Fund our Future

If Watford Palace Theatre and what it represents are important to you, please consider supporting us with a gift in your Will.

Whether you are a supporter of our work on stage, have an interest in engaging young people through theatre, or would simply like to support the Palace as a whole, we hope that you will consider remembering us with a gift in your Will.

Your most personal and lasting gift can be of any size; every donation helps and no amount is too small. By leaving a legacy you will be helping future audiences to discover the wonder of theatre and enjoy Watford Palace as you do today.

Watford Palace's charitable status may offer you the opportunity to reduce the tax due on your estate.

For further information please contact our Development Team on 01923 257472 or alternatively email development@watfordpalacetheatre.co.uk

Thank you for considering this special gesture.

Thank you to the members of the Green Room Donors Club for their generous support:

Gold Members
Dr Lewis Farrow
Mrs T Kealey
Mr Clive Payne
Mr John Perry
Mr P Richardson
Mrs J Ryder
Mrs Adele Taylor
Mr Waterton
Mr Philip White

Silver Members
Mrs M Brown
Mrs Pamela Brown
Mrs L Cotes
Mrs Valerie Dutton
Mr & Mrs FH & P Fordham
Mr D Gibney
Mr K Gooch
Mrs Pat Hiscock
Dr Eva Hnizdo
Mr Ian Laidlaw-Dickson
Mrs Janet Landau
Mrs R Moore
Ms Helen Payne
Mrs S Stalley
Mr Mark Watkin

Staff List

BOARD OF DIRECTORS
Deborah Lincoln (Chair)
Alex Bottom
Tola Dabiri
Cllr. George Derbyshire
John Hunt
Beverley Jullien
Sneha Khilay
Alok Mitra
Patricia Munn
Emma O'Connor
Brett Spencer
Patrick Stoddart
Amber Townsend
Gary Townsend Vila

Artistic Director and Chief Executive
Brigid Larmour

Communications Director
Dan Baxter

Executive Producer
Jamie Arden

OPERATIONS Producer
Harriet Mackie

Administrator/ PA to the Executive Team
Samantha Ford

Maintenance Technician
Brian Penston

Head of Finance
Andrew Phillips

Finance Officer
Tatiana Tiberghien

CUSTOMER SERVICES Manager
Amy Platt

Customer Services Manager (Maternity Cover)
Sheryl Southall

Front of House & Bar Manager
Allen Gray

Cleaning Supervisor
Sharon Hunt

Cleaning Staff
Craig Ewer
Mohammed Fahim
Ankomah Koduah
Christina Pavely

PARTICIPATION Head of Participation
Kirsten Hutton

Resident Director (Participation)
James Williams

Participation Projects Manager
Nicole Artingstall

PRODUCTION Head of Production
Matt Ledbury

Head of Electrics
Richmond Rudd

Deputy Head of Electrics
Francis Johnstone

Technician
Daniel Frost

Stage Technician
Chris Taylor

Head of Construction
Tip Pargeter

Construction Assistant
Phil Atherton

MARKETING AND SALES Marketing and Press Officer
Vanessa White

Marketing and Press Officer
Kerry Manning

Marketing and Press Assistant
Cerys Beesley

Sales & Membership Supervisor
Julia Yelland

Sales & Membership Assistants
Sophie Sellars
Peter Shelton

CUSTOMER SERVICE TEAM
Morgan Bebbington
Ella Brightley
William Burchnall
Myles Connaghan
Luis Connolly
David Cox
AD Dada
Kenny Dada
Tai Dada
Olivia Davies
Hannah Draper
Amy Duncan
Rory Duncan
James Dyer
Hope Feasey
Bev Fisher
Clare Floyd
Lauren Foreman
David Gigney
Meridian Griffiths
James Grout
Tamsin Harding
Rosie Hess
Kirsty Henley-Washford
Ben Henley-Washford
Mac Hughes
Robbie Hunt
Sasha Iqbal
Mia Janes
Johanna Coraline Jensen
Jeanette Johnson
Brandon Jones
Holly Jones
Elaine Kaye
Josh Kelly
Sarah Kenny
Fynn Levy
Calum Littley
Laurelle Marfleet
Lewis Marshall
Saul Masters
Alicia McKay
Paul Mead
Grace Meyer
Hannah Miller
Rebecca Milton
Jess Moss
Teresa Murray
Isabel Neilson
George O'Dell
Madeline O'Keeffe
Harriet O'Neill
Alice O'Shaughnessy
Emily Pardoe
Michael Pitt
Mark Pocock
Rita Reidy

Chloe Robinson Hunter
Annie Robson
Elliot Rosen
Valerie Sadoh
Tom Scarborough
Sam Selby-Weatherley
Janet Semus
Layla Savage
Ellie Shrimpton-Ring
Olympia Shodipo
Utkarsh Singh
Natalie Spencer
Charlotte Spencer
Charlotte Wallis
Chloe May Ware
Jack Whitney
Imara Williams-Simpson
Tom Wilson
Joseph Winer
Emily Withers

Honorary Archivist
Ian Scleater

CREATIVE ASSOCIATES Resident Companies
Rifco, Tiata Fahodzi

Companies
Scamp, Mahogany Opera Group

Writers
Alice Birch,
Stacey Gregg,
Charlotte Keatley,
Gary Owen,
Timberlake Wertenbaker

Choreography/ Movement
Kate Flatt, Shona Morris

Watford Palace Theatre is a registered Charity No.1056950

POPPY + GEORGE

Diane Samuels

Acknowledgements

Many thanks to all at Watford Palace Theatre, especially Brigid Larmour, Harriet Mackie, Dan Baxter, Samantha Ford, for wonderful teamwork and bringing this play to new life and light; to family constellations therapist Gaye Donaldson for probing group explorations into the character and story; to Niamh Cusack at Rose Bruford and to open-hearted volunteers for development workshop, Jasper Hardcastle, Charlotte Slater, James Nickerson, Corinne Powesland, Anna Panzone, Charlotte Tayler; to insightful and skilful actors at development workshops, Ken Christiansen, Samantha Robinson, Anna O'Grady, Terence Frisch; to my trusty agent Caroline Underwood for support and expertise and all at Alan Brodie Representation; to inspired composer, musician and friend Gwyneth Herbert; to director Jennie Darnell for her remarkable insight, warmth and rigour; to Lucy Barrett for invaluable back-up; to actors Mark Rice-Oxley, Rebecca Oldfield, Jacob Krichefski and Nadia Clifford for breathing true life into every written word; to Ruari Murchison for his expertise, imagination and practicality; to Emma Hansford, Emma Ryan and Maddie Baylis for doing all they do; to Ben and Jake Garfield, my beloved sons, for love, insights and simply being themselves; to Paul Berrill for love, support and care on many levels.

To Julie Wheelwright and her book *Amazons and Military Maids* and all at Theatre Centre, young people's theatre in the early 1990s, especially Becky Chapman, Isobel Hawson and Rosamunde Hutt, and Karen Spicer, Ivan Heng, Jess Charles, Robin Samson, Maria McAteer, Hazel Maycock.

D.S.

'In Flanders fields the poppies blow
Between the crosses, row on row.'

'In Flanders Fields'
John McCrae

'Gentle sleep! Scatter thy drowsiest poppies from above
And in new dreams not soon to vanish, bless
My senses with the sight of her I love.'

'Poppies and Sleep'
Horace Smith

4

Characters

POPPY WRIGHT, *modern young woman from the north of England. Early twenties.*
TOMMY JOHNS, *music-hall artiste. Musician. Around forty.*
SMITH, *tailor and dressmaker. Jewish-Russian origin. Well-travelled. Fifties or maybe older.*
GEORGE SAMPSON, *chauffeur. Late twenties/early thirties.*

Note on Play

The play is set entirely in Smith's tailor and costumier's workshop in the East End of London in 1919.

Whilst the script refers to Tommy playing the piano, it is highly possible that he might play another instrument that is fitting for his music-hall genre, e.g. ukulele, accordion, glockenspiel, triangle, etc.

A glossary is provided on page 103.

This text went to press before the end of rehearsals and so may differ slightly from the play as performed.

Scene One

The Maid

Wind stirs.

Echoes of 'After the War is Over'.

A tailor and costumier's workshop.

Here are dummies and a bizarre range of outfits in many different stages of creation. Uniforms hang by Japanese kimonos by Elizabethan hose by saris by corsets by togas and more.

There are a couple of sewing machines and an old upright piano too.

TOMMY *stands still. He is wearing a half-made maid's uniform.*

SMITH *is adjusting and pinning the outfit. He wears a Chinese Zhongshan suit and shirt.*

GEORGE *is wearing full chauffeur uniform and is searching through a basket of various shirts.*

TOMMY. How about Charlotte?

GEORGE. Nah.

SMITH. What kind of girl are you after?

TOMMY. The ordinary kind?… But with a touch… oh, you know… a touch of something else?

SMITH. Coarse or refined?

TOMMY. Not sure.

GEORGE. You slowing down, Tom?

TOMMY. Give us a chance.

GEORGE. Thought you could knock off a little maid no problem.

TOMMY. Some girls can be tricky, you know.

SMITH. Is it her or is it you?

TOMMY. You think I'm losing my nerve?

SMITH. You had a bit of a break, Tommy.

TOMMY. And what in heaven's name have I come back to?

GEORGE. Hey now, what about the tiddley iddleys?

SMITH. Tiddley iddleys?

GEORGE. Come on, Tom, show him how you kept the home fires alight in all our hearts.

SMITH. Well?

> TOMMY *groans, then sings some of 'Take Me Back to Dear Old Blighty'.*

TOMMY (*sings*).
> Tiddley iddley ighty
> Carry me back to Blighty
> Blighty is the place for me…
> Lousy bloody peace.

SMITH. *Der ergster sholem…*

TOMMY. Sorry, don't speak Chinese, my friend.

SMITH. The worst peace is better…

GEORGE.…than the best war.

SMITH. See, he listens to me.

TOMMY. But where, pray, does a man even begin?

GEORGE. Where does any man begin with a girl?

TOMMY. At a loss.

GEORGE. Look, don't worry yourself about the whole of her. Just find her name and the rest'll follow.

TOMMY. So what's wrong with Charlotte!

GEORGE. Too bookish.

SMITH. He's got a point.

TOMMY. Petunia?

GEORGE. Too prissy.

TOMMY. How about you do her instead, George?

GEORGE. I'm no good at girls.

TOMMY. Sounds like you're the bloomin' expert.

GEORGE. No one does a lady like you.

TOMMY. Did, George. Did.

GEORGE. Keep at her and she'll come.

TOMMY. Give over.

SMITH. Turn around, please.

    TOMMY *turns and* SMITH *continues pinning.*

GEORGE. Smith, how long do I have to hang around here
    before we sort this shirt?

SMITH. *Bing dong san chi…*

TOMMY. Ah, three feet of ice is not formed in a single day.

SMITH. So you do speak Chinese.

TOMMY. I listen too, see.

GEORGE. What you on about?

TOMMY. Patience, my friend, patience.

GEORGE. Does this mean, Smith, that you're going to spend
    the entire afternoon pinning old Mrs Skivvy Pants over there?

TOMMY. Mrs Skivvy Pants? OLD Mrs Skivvy Pants! What
    kind of artist do you think I am?

SMITH. Keep still.

TOMMY. This godawful act's doing me in. I swear it on my dear Bessie's grave.

GEORGE. Your Bessie's still alive, Tom.

TOMMY. She won't be after she's seen the state of this little number.

GEORGE. What about Henrietta?

TOMMY. Not common enough.

SMITH. Common girl. Posh name. Might that, with respect, be 'the gag'?

TOMMY. Huppity Henrietta...

SMITH. Ah now perhaps she is in your sights.

TOMMY. The hunder-parlour maid.

SMITH. How buxom?

TOMMY. If in doubt...

SMITH. ...pad her out.

TOMMY. More stuffing, maestro?

SMITH. My feelings precisely.

TOMMY. Better get me kit off then...

   SMITH *searches for stuffing.*

   TOMMY *starts to undo the buttons down the front of the dress.*

   Winds of change blow.

   Musical theme as...

   POPPY *enters, neatly dressed, carrying a small bag.*

GEORGE (*to* POPPY). Hello.

TOMMY. Whoopsie daisy!

   He closes his blouse with a flourish of modesty.

POPPY. I'm looking for a Mr Smith.

SMITH. I am Smith.

POPPY. Oh phew for that. All them passageways and turns and lost track entirely of whether I was going round in circles or backwards or forwards or sideways any more… So this is it, is it?

SMITH. If this is indeed where you were heading, then it appears that with all success you have arrived.

SMITH *and* POPPY *shake hands.*

POPPY. Pleased to meet you, Mr Smith.

SMITH. Just Smith.

GEORGE *stands up and holds out a hand.*

GEORGE. George Sampson. As in Delilah.

POPPY *looks a bit confused but nods in acknowledgement.*

TOMMY. Tommy Johns. (*Bowing.*) As in long.

POPPY *looks bemused.*

Think about it.

POPPY. Oh. Ahhh…

TOMMY. Delighted to make your h-acquaintance.

SMITH. Tommy is a performer.

GEORGE. Top of the bill.

TOMMY. So to speak.

SMITH. Do you wish to hire, buy or order?

POPPY. To be hired, I hope.

SMITH. You are a seamstress?

POPPY. I wouldn't say… I mean, yes I can sew well enough…

SMITH. You consider yourself to be more than what you do for a living.

POPPY. Oh. You understand.

SMITH. After entering this establishment did you close the front door behind you?

POPPY. Maybe left it a bit ajar…

GEORGE. I'll check.

GEORGE *nips out*.

POPPY. Couldn't find a knocker, and it pushed to, so I walked in.

SMITH. An unlocked door is as an unlocked mind… as long as we take care… All who come in pursuit of genuine business are welcome.

POPPY. I was told you're looking for assistance.

SMITH. References?

POPPY *gets out her references and samplers and hands them to* SMITH.

POPPY. I can do all the basics. Me mam taught me. Used to mend and make for me brother and sisters.

GEORGE *reappears, he carries a package*.

GEORGE. Door good… And Cheng popped in to give you this… If you still want the brocade, he said, meet him at Paddy's Corner tomorrow morning before eight.

SMITH *nods to place the package with some others*. GEORGE *does so*.

SMITH (*reading*). Mary Louisa Wright.

TOMMY. Modest Mary?… Melodious Mary?… Holy Mary?

POPPY. I like to be called Poppy.

SMITH. Does anyone else call you Poppy?

POPPY. I'm not answering if they don't.

TOMMY. Proud Poppy? Plucky Poppy? Perfectly principled Poppy?

POPPY (*to* TOMMY). D'you mind me asking, sir, what you're on about?

TOMMY. Just exploring the possibilities... that suddenly seem to be presenting themselves...

POPPY. What possibilities?

SMITH. Are you conscientious?

POPPY. It says there about the quality of me work...

TOMMY. A poppy outstanding in her field.

GEORGE. Give a girl a chance, Tom.

TOMMY. I am. I am.

SMITH. I have just sent a girl packing because she fell short.

POPPY. I hope, Mr Smith...

SMITH. What is the English problem? I choose the commonest name in your language, make it even simpler by removing the title and still you cannot get it right.

POPPY. It's the way we've been taught, see.

SMITH. Make the effort, in this instance, to unteach yourself. If you call me mister again, Poppy, or, for that matter, sir, then I will call you Mary.

POPPY. I understand.

SMITH. Good. At last. Someone who really does understand.

POPPY. I do hope that I will not disappoint you.

TOMMY. Then don't be sloppy, Poppy.

GEORGE. How come you left your last position?

POPPY. It's a delicate matter.

TOMMY. We are all delicate men here, my dear.

POPPY. It's just... my mistress took offence.

SMITH. Did you misbehave?

TOMMY. Get into a spot of trouble?

POPPY. I did not.

SMITH. Did you question her authority?

TOMMY. Raise your head a little too high?

POPPY. I didn't ask her to tell me.

TOMMY. Pray tell us.

POPPY. All I was doing was hanging the kiddies' new jackets
and she just says… Oh never mind.

GEORGE. Go on. What she say to you?

POPPY. I mean it started happily enough…

TOMMY. Doesn't it always. I mean, with my wife…

SMITH. You were hanging the jackets?

POPPY. And she says, 'Isn't that dear of you to embroider
Charlie's dogs on his collar.'

SMITH. His dogs embroidered on a child's collar. Interesting
touch.

POPPY. Scottie dogs, they were… with the waggy tail and all…

TOMMY (*sings*).
　　Daddy wouldn't buy me a bow-wow!
　　Daddy wouldn't buy me a bow-wow…

SMITH. So she liked the embroidery…

TOMMY (*sings*).
　　Bow-wow.

POPPY. And I says that he's one of the sweetest lads I ever come
across. And… Oh it's truly not of any real consequence.

TOMMY (*sings*).
　　I've got a little cat
　　And I'm very fond of that…

GEORGE. Did you mean it, about her kid?

POPPY. I did. I really meant it. Loved him to bits, her little lad.

TOMMY (*sings*).
> But I'd rather have a bow-wow
> Wow wow wow wow...

GEORGE. Touched a nerve, did ya?

POPPY. Stirred her right up... On and on she's going 'bout
Charlie being her 'child of hope', coming along after the
master had gone missing in action and then being found.

GEORGE. No harm done there, is there?

POPPY. Then she draws me in. Asks if I know what it's like to
think you've lost everything then have it miraculously
restored.

GEORGE. And do you?

POPPY. Should have stopped me mouth, but do I ever? And
now I'm splurgin' too, like a waterfall, 'bout me teacher,
Miss Pembridge... How she got struck by pneumonia and
was at death's door. And how I'll never forget the day she
come back into us classroom and says, 'I am so pleased to be
with you all.' I even told her how we clapped and cheered
and I cried for joy.

GEORGE. What you clapping for when she was just your
teacher?

SMITH. So you told all this to your mistress?

POPPY. And got myself all tearful too... So we're working
each other up to a froth... and she's suddenly blurting that
she didn't realise there'd never be another like the master,
not until she thought she'd lost him... and when he came
back something in the way inside just lifted. And the day
they made little Charlie... all in a passion like she'd never
felt before... she'd lain herself flat on the ground and given
herself to him in the stables. And I goes and asks her why
she wanted to lay down on the ground for anyone. And she
says, 'Because that's what you do when you truly love a
man.' And I says... It sounds less like love and... I should
have kept me trap shut...

GEORGE. Less like love?

POPPY. …and more like slavery.

> TOMMY, GEORGE *and* SMITH *exchange glances*.
>
> And the mistress goes stiff as an icicle. Then she walks out.
>
> Next day Mr Proctor, head butler, hands me the references coz my services are no longer required.

TOMMY. Presumptious Poppy.

POPPY. I was being honest and she was with me and what's so very wrong, I ask you, with that? Are we not both women with feelings all the same?

GEORGE. Never kid yourself you can be familiar with them up there.

POPPY. I'm never going into service ever again. Wouldn't have done it in the first place if me mam hadn't gone on and on at us.

> TOMMY *sits at the piano and starts to play around with some tunes*.

TOMMY. So, Poppy my peach, you've escaped the servant's quarters and run off down to the Big Smoke to work in the sweatshops instead, have you?

GEORGE. How long are you planning on staying?

POPPY. I'm not going back. Why should I, to being nagged and nagged till I get wed? And I don't care if she never writes to me again. She needn't. And she doesn't have to let me know about whether my little sister gets better, either. Why should I do the same as her and her mother before just because… just because…?

SMITH. Because they did?

POPPY. And I was told that you would appreciate a girl like me…

TOMMY. Well, who on earth wouldn't?

POPPY....with my skills and attitude.

SMITH. Who told you this?

POPPY. A friend of Miss Pembridge... who's been letting me
lodge with her for a bit... you know, helping her out... But
she's having her baby soon... and I told her I don't want to
nanny... And she said that you had lodgings here too... and
you might need an assistant... See her letter... you know,
Mrs Lloyd...

SMITH *looks at the papers again.*

SMITH. Ah yes... A lady of modest means and great style.

GEORGE. Will you take her on?

TOMMY *starts trying out a tune on the piano.*

TOMMY. How about... something like...

(*Sings.*)
H-I am something to look at, a pleasure to 'ear
'Enrietta h-I'm called, h-understand?
And all 'ousehold problems disperse when h-I'm near
With me little feather duster in me 'and.

GEORGE. You made that up quick.

TOMMY. Funny, isn't it. A bit of new blood... and what do you
know... the old wheels crank into motion... Thank you,
Poppy.

POPPY. What have I done?

TOMMY. Don't mind being an old trouper's muse, do you?

POPPY. Pardon, but it's not my intention to amuse anyone...

TOMMY. Look, she speaks, and I can't help myself...

(*Sings.*)
The master and mistress were right out of sort
'Is 'orses were far out to grass...

Out it just pops...

POPPY. But I'm not doing anything!

TOMMY (*sings*).

> But 'e soon rediscovered the meaning of sport
> With me little feather duster up...

POPPY. What's this got to do with me!

TOMMY (*sings*).

> The 'ead nursery governess, madam to you
> Could work out every difficult sum
> But h-I taught 'er new ways one and one can make two
> With me little feather duster up 'er...

POPPY. Smith. Sir. Please can you...

TOMMY (*sings*).

> H-old Proctor the butler was well past 'is prime
> What with 'is totters and falls
> So h-I got up behind 'im and lengthened 'is time...
> With me little...

POPPY. Please tell me. Have I got the job, sir?

SMITH. As long as you never call me sir ever again.

POPPY. You're on.

They shake on it.

TOMMY (*sings*).

> 'Oo says there's a problem with servants these days?
> That we've all lost our place in these lands?
> We'll sort out h-all manner of h-uppity ways
> With our little feather dusters
> Our fluffy feather dusters
> With our little feather dusters in our 'ands.

Feather-duster motif becomes faster and faster.

The basket of shirts that GEORGE *had been sifting through is hurled into the air and white and black shirts pour out here, there and everywhere...*

Scene Two

Wheels

Rhythm of folding methodically.

SMITH*'s workshop theme in a major key.*

POPPY *folds and piles each shirt, one by one, very carefully.*

SMITH *is selecting a number of paper patterns from the shelf or chest of drawers where many more are also kept.*

He lays out the patterns on a large mat on the floor.

SMITH. Fore body. Two pieces – right side and left…

POPPY. Might I ask you something, Mist… I mean, Smith?

SMITH. Side parts… Back… You might.

POPPY. Were you born in China?

SMITH. I was not… Shoulder heads…?

POPPY. Did you grow up there then?

SMITH. I grew up in Russia… the Pale part where they herded the Jews… Yes, shoulder heads…

POPPY. So how comes…?

SMITH. War, Poppy… It was the war with China that set me off… It's a hungry beast, the Russian army, gobbling up young men to keep it on its feet.

POPPY. Can't imagine you a soldier.

SMITH. Neither could I… which is why, like you… I escaped.

POPPY. Deserted?

SMITH. If that's what they want to call it, they may… But, for my part, I was searching for the source of the Silk Road… which led me to the court of the Emperor Gu… where I found the master tailor who taught me his ancient craft… remarkable years… until he made the fatal error… of stepping out of line…

POPPY. In what way?

SMITH. A lady, my dear.

POPPY. Oh.

SMITH. One of the Emperor's ladies. So he never saw light of day again.

POPPY. Gosh.

SMITH. There have been other masters of other crafts since… and many miles following my own feet… but he was the first… perhaps the finest…

POPPY. You still miss him?

SMITH. What a teacher writes on the blackboard of your life can never be erased… Now, Poppy, can you come here please.

POPPY *stops folding and joins him.*

SMITH *holds up pieces of pattern around her to visualise the garment.*

Shoulder heads, yes… Straps… and fasten to the fore body… Side-waisted or short-waisted?… Short… Yes… Stomacher… To be open behind… How many eyelet holes?… Aha… Wood or whalebone?… No no… I think the metal…

POPPY. What is this – a corset or a straitjacket?

SMITH. The design is seventeenth century. French.

POPPY. They were barbaric in them days.

SMITH. Has much changed?

POPPY. I should hope so. And if it hasn't, it's time it did.

SMITH. Do times change because we make them or do we change because they make us?

POPPY. Is it for Tommy?

SMITH. A proper actress… in Molière.

POPPY. Don't actresses have to breathe?

SMITH. How do you breathe in yours?

POPPY. Well, there's no metal or wood for starters. Anyhow, I loosen the stays to please myself, see.

SMITH. Well, this is for a mistress of her craft who insists upon the authentic thing... I can loosen the shoulder straps a little, and some chamois will ease the rubbing on the armpits... But the shape, the shape must hold. In this its splendour lies.

GEORGE *enters looking spick and span. He carries a sack and a box.*

GEORGE. How is life treating you this merry morn?

SMITH. Could be better...

GEORGE/SMITH. Could be worse.

GEORGE. Your ribbons and bows, milud.

SMITH *receives the sack and checks inside.*

And here's a little something that's looking for a home.

He hands the box to SMITH.

SMITH *looks inside.*

Kodak black-box camera Brownie 2, Model E, that is... And the other's a candlestick telephone... rotary dial and all...

SMITH. You shouldn't have.

SMITH *looks with interest and nods approvingly.*

George has come to collect his shirt, Poppy.

SMITH *carefully closes and puts away the box.*

POPPY *searches the piles.*

GEORGE *picks up a black shirt.*

POPPY. Those are for the Anarchists.

GEORGE. What do you know about Anarchists?

POPPY. Only what Smith said about how society is perfectly able to exist without any government at all.

GEORGE. What else have you been telling her?

SMITH. Those who are curious deserve a response.

POPPY. What does liberty mean to you, George?

GEORGE (*putting it down*). You want to watch it, Smith...

SMITH. Oh, I watch...

GEORGE. Watch out, putting yourself... and others... in any kind of peril...

SMITH. And how colourful the peril is these days... Red peril, black peril, brown peril...

GEORGE. Yellow Peril, they're calling, down by the docks... now the demobs are back... D'you not hear the ruckus about look who's got our jobs now? Have you seen the size of Mr Chan's black eye?

SMITH. Oh I hear. I heed. And even when... *especially* when... the old stiches now unstitch and the world comes apart at the seams... someone has to cut and tack and pick and unpick and keep the needle moving somehow, don't they, to keep us all from falling apart.

POPPY *presents a folded white shirt.*

POPPY. This is yours.

GEORGE *looks it over.*

GEORGE. Very fine.

POPPY *sets to wrapping the shirt in brown paper.*

SMITH *puts aside the corset and turns to sewing some Cossack trousers.*

D'you know what I did yesterday?

POPPY. Went to church?

GEORGE. After that.

POPPY. Lunch.

GEORGE. After that.

POPPY. Perhaps you forgot something.

GEORGE. Did I?

POPPY. Smith said you said you'd pop by yesterday for this. I was up early adjusting it for you.

GEORGE. Were you?

POPPY. Some of us have a job to do, you know, and whole piles to get through and I would've put it off if I'd known.

GEORGE. Well, I would've come yesterday, only I had to polish my autos.

POPPY. *Your* autos?

GEORGE. Nothing compares to a Silver Ghost. 'Slipper Flywheel' vibration damper. Twin-jet carburettor with governor to maintain road speed. Four-speed gearbox with direct-drive fourth. Footbrake with rear drums. Forty to fifty horsepower. And, the pièce de résistance, as his dear Lordship loves telling fellow passengers, electric starting and lighting.

POPPY. You're a lucky man to do a job you love so well.

GEORGE. We're all lucky men. Look at us, with our wits about us and all our parts intact.

SMITH. Is it luck we have to thank?

GEORGE. When Fortune holds out her hand, be the one to grab it.

SMITH. No one is luckier than he who believes in his luck.

POPPY. Luck never gives, it only lends.

GEORGE. By the grace of God, there goes I.

POPPY *presents the wrapped shirt.*

POPPY. Your shirt is ready, Mr Sampson.

GEORGE (*taking the package*). Good girl. (*To* SMITH.) Got your lace still in the car, Smith.

SMITH. You had better go and get it then.

GEORGE exits.

POPPY. Pardon me for asking, but does Mr Sampson often have shirts made for him?

SMITH. Now and then.

Pause. Silence. They work.

POPPY. What about other items for his wardrobe?

SMITH. The occasional jacket. The odd pair of trousers. His uniforms.

POPPY. How many does he have?

SMITH. Two for normal wear. One for special.

Pause. Silence. They work.

POPPY. Does he regularly do chores for you?

SMITH. Then and now.

POPPY. And are there other occasions when he…?

SMITH. Occasions do occur when he recurs, yes.

POPPY. Oh?

SMITH. And they might involve the odd dram or shuffle of the cards.

POPPY. Ah.

SMITH. Do you ever indulge?

POPPY. I'm not a gambling woman.

GEORGE enters. He is carrying a pile of packages.

GEORGE. Where d'you want them?

SMITH indicates. GEORGE has taken off his jacket and his sleeves are rolled up. He puts away the parcels.

POPPY *watches* GEORGE. *She stares at a large scar on one of his arms.*

POPPY (*looking away*). Pardon me.

GEORGE. Ah, it's nothing.

POPPY. How d'you get it?

GEORGE. Nabbed a villain and he slashed me.

POPPY. Oooh.

GEORGE. Tell a lie. Got into a fight with an escaped tiger at the zoo.

POPPY. What really happened?

GEORGE. Take your pick.

POPPY. No. Really.

GEORGE. Well, when you're groping in the dark...

POPPY. Go on.

GEORGE. ...trying to carry a stretcher and all... you can miss the odd barb of wire... or whatever's got shattered and sharp... Lucky I'm nippy on me feet.

POPPY. Must have hurt.

GEORGE. Never feel it at the time, anyhow... Got off lightly.

POPPY. Left its mark alright.

GEORGE. Adds character though, eh?

POPPY. You reckon?

POPPY *concentrates on the sewing.* SMITH *also sews.* GEORGE *comes and sits next to* POPPY.

GEORGE. Did your mum write to you then in the end?

POPPY. Got a letter beginning of the week.

GEORGE. All straightened out between you now?

POPPY. She reckons I'll be back before the month's out.

GEORGE. Is she right?

POPPY. Wishful thinking.

GEORGE. And your little sister, is she better?

POPPY. Gracie? A lot better, thanks. She sent me her kisses.

GEORGE. Miss her, do you?

POPPY. Goes both ways.

GEORGE. Gets easier.

POPPY. Our Katie can plait Gracie's hair as well as I ever did. I daresay she'll get over it.

GEORGE. No brothers?

POPPY. Only Danny.

GEORGE. Older? Younger?

POPPY. He's the babby. Nearly ten now.

GEORGE. Full of beans?

POPPY. Bright as a button. He's the one called me Poppy.

GEORGE. How come?

POPPY. I used to grow them in pots on our front ledge – red, orange, even yellow ones. Cheer the place up. When he was a tiddler, I'd show him how to do the planting and watering. And I'd tell him the secret of their seeds, how they lie, maybe even for years, sleeping in the soil, but always alive, waiting for the earth to be upset to wake them up and let them grow.

GEORGE. Is that right?

POPPY. It is. Yes. Anyhow, it was our thing together, our little Danny and me. And he'd pick some and plant them in my hair, like, for me to wear. I loved that.

GEORGE. Poppy suits you.

POPPY. You think so?

GEORGE. I do.

POPPY. What about your family?

GEORGE. Four brothers, three sisters and only one bicycle between the lot of us… Oh hey, d'you know what I saw yesterday?

POPPY. What d'you see?

GEORGE. A tandem.

POPPY. Oh?

GEORGE. And I thought, 'I could do with one of them.'

POPPY. What d'you want with a tandem when you've got an auto?

GEORGE. Four autos.

POPPY. What does anyone need that many for?

GEORGE. Each one's entirely different.

POPPY. Is it?

GEORGE. Anyhow, autos do one thing, this tandem'd do another.

POPPY. How?

GEORGE. Good to get the legs going with someone behind you.

POPPY. You always go at the front, do you?

GEORGE. Back too, sometimes. For a laugh.

POPPY. Which d'you prefer?

GEORGE. Driving seat, of course.

POPPY. You can't do the brakes on the back.

GEORGE. Always got to keep your hands on the brakes, have you?

POPPY. Maybe.

GEORGE. I've jumped over ditches on tandems before now.

POPPY. You can't. They're too heavy.

GEORGE. Not if you both pedal like the clappers.

POPPY. Who d'you do it with?

GEORGE. Only those with nerves as strong as their legs.

POPPY. Anyone in particular?

GEORGE. So shall I borrow a tandem?

POPPY. What's it got to do with me?

GEORGE. You're the one I'm wanting to take out for a ride.

POPPY. I s'pose I could do with some fresh air.

GEORGE. So, it's a cycle in the country, is it?

POPPY. Is it?

GEORGE. Well?

POPPY. Don't see why not.

GEORGE. You working this Saturday?

POPPY. Whole day off.

GEORGE. Pick you up in the morning?

POPPY. What'll we do if it rains?

GEORGE. Get wet.

POPPY. I knew you'd say that.

GEORGE. Fingers crossed, eh?

POPPY. And toes.

GEORGE. See you then.

POPPY. See you.

GEORGE. Ta-ta for now.

　　GEORGE *goes*.

POPPY *continues to sew.*

SMITH *holds up the trousers (full-cut, gathered at the waistband and made from unbleached linen), shakes them out and examines them.*

SMITH *(adjusting and pinning).* Cossack trousers. The English version. Introduced in 1814 when the Czar came to London for the peace celebrations.

POPPY. Why must you make everything so accurate?

SMITH. Why do a thing at all if not perfectly?

POPPY. But what is the point of copying clothes that no one wears any more for people who pretend to be what they're not?

SMITH. Why should anyone want to jump a tandem over a ditch?

POPPY. Pardon, but that's my private business.

SMITH. So it is.

POPPY. Please don't think that I don't respect the very high… well, highest quality of all you make… On my life, I never saw such skill and garments before…

SMITH. You are not without skill yourself, Poppy.

POPPY. I've had enough practice to get by.

SMITH. More than that. You have the eye. You have the feel. You have the… shall we say, imaginative passion… to develop true artisty.

POPPY. What're you on about?

SMITH. Apply yourself utterly, devote all your time and attention to developing the expertise and you have it in you to make your mark… if not a very good living… maybe even as a master tailor… as I do.

POPPY. I could never ever be anywhere near as good as you are.

SMITH. Let me guide you and you will be become far far better than you think you can be.

POPPY. You have that much faith in me?

SMITH. From the moment you described embroidering the dogs on the little boy's collar.

POPPY. I did love doing that.

SMITH. Discipline and devotion is required, of course, for an assistant to become an apprentice.

POPPY. I'm not afraid of hard work.

SMITH. Putting in extra hours.

POPPY. You mean, on my days off?

SMITH. Starting forthwith.

POPPY. Forthwith?

SMITH. Why wait?

POPPY. Well. Oh my. I'm honoured... Most honoured... but the truth is... sewing and tailoring and fashioning might be your way in the world... but, with the greatest respect, if I'd wanted to end up sewing, I might as well've stayed at home. And anyhow, when did you ever see a master tailor wearing a skirt?

SMITH. In China, India, Arabia...

POPPY. Women all?

SMITH. You spoke of a skirt not the manner of person inside it, Poppy.

POPPY. You know what I mean.

SMITH. Want to try these on for size?

POPPY. I'm no Cossack. Not even the English kind. And thank you... but truth be told I want my time off for... well... for myself... and to go out and all...

SMITH. Are you sure?

POPPY. And truly, I'm no tailor.

SMITH. Then tell me, who do you want to be?

POPPY. You mean, what do I want to do?

SMITH. If you like.

POPPY. Well... I want to get more skills to me name, I know that... Make my own way and not be having always to answer to someone else... To be independent like, on my own two feet... comfortable even in my own skin... Not to have to wear a uniform... or even if I could a corset ever again... That'd be nice. And being useful, you know... Making a difference... To study if I felt the urge, even a girl like me. Miss Pembridge said that I had it in me... She said I could become anything I set my mind to... Not sure about anything... but still... something...

SMITH. I have learned, Poppy, that once you step out of the world that you thought was all-embracing, you realise that you can choose to step into any world you please.

POPPY. How does that work?

SMITH. Which world do you wish to enter? In what form?

He opens his arms, offering every costume in the entire workshop.

Take your pick.

POPPY. No matter what goes on top, I am what I am. And my skin's rough. You'd never make it fine, not even with a million yards of the most precious cloth.

SMITH. Do you want to be the dummy or the tailor?

POPPY. How am I a dummy?

SMITH. Either you are fashioned by what you're told or think you're told you can be... or you dare to fashion yourself.

POPPY. What's the point in pretending to be a silk purse?

SMITH. Pretend it and believe it.

POPPY. Why would I want to?

SMITH. What if you discovered that you might start to believe it… and not only that… everybody else believes it too?

SMITH's theme stirs.

POPPY. That doesn't make it true?

SMITH. Why not?

The music becomes stronger.

SMITH raises the Cossack trousers on high to the strains of the music.

POPPY tentatively starts to turn and allow the music to surge through her.

SMITH watches, fascinated, something stirring within him too.

Scene Three

Mary + Qwerty

Fragment of Mary waltz.

TOMMY wears men's underwear and sits by a tub of water. He washes himself.

Around him are strewn a variety of women's outfits emerging from an old suitcase.

TOMMY (*little-girl voice*). 'Where can it be?'

Buggered if I know.

'But how will I manage without it?'

Where have you looked?

'Nowhere to be seen.'

Must be somewhere.

He scrubs hard.

Must be. Mustn't it. Somewhere?

He goes over each place he has washed a number of times. It is as if he can't get himself clean.

POPPY *enters. She is wearing a coat and hat and carries a newspaper.*

POPPY. Here again, Mr Johns?

TOMMY. Me and Bessie's had one of our barnies, love.

POPPY. I have to get myself changed.

TOMMY. Don't mind me. She doesn't.

POPPY. Nothing I can get you?

TOMMY. Seen a sheep knocking about?

POPPY. Only the cow at the dairy down the road.

TOMMY. It's about so high... fluffy... well, woolly... White... well, yellowing... bleats if you press it in the right place.

POPPY. Oh... Well, there's a rug somewhere... I think that's made of some kind of fleece...

TOMMY. Not a rug no. It's a sheep. It's got legs... well, wheels...

POPPY. What's it for?

TOMMY *picks up a stiff piece of rope.*

TOMMY. Attached to this, see?... So it followed... close behind...

He illustrates walking and turning with a sheep attached on the rope behind him.

And when I turned... it moved with me... So I couldn't spot it, right?... But everyone else could... See?

POPPY. Behind you?

TOMMY. Exactly. Behind me!

POPPY. Sorry, I don't think I have seen it.

TOMMY. She used to go down well... previously... Quite lost track of her... Lost track of all sorts... don't realise the half of it... Until you go through the old cozzies...

He holds up a shepherdess outfit.

You're not the only one, love, who used to be a Mary.

POPPY. Well, I'm not any more.

TOMMY. You are, really...

POPPY. Nor did I go to school looking like a milkmaid!

TOMMY. Shepherdess, if you don't mind...

POPPY. That neither. Now I really must...

POPPY *gets off her coat and shoes, etc.*

TOMMY. Yep. Get ready. Don't worry yerself...

TOMMY *finds and takes up his ukulele, adorned with lambs and pastoral illustrations.*

Still, she might need some patching-up and making fresh again... Coz she has to be fresh, does little Mary, don't you agree?... Hey... (*Sniffing at his skin.*) You can't smell anything in here, can you?

POPPY. Just the usual damp and rot.

TOMMY. Cloying... like... mud... it smells of to me.

POPPY. Slum smell. It's not human.

TOMMY. All too human, me dear...

POPPY *looks through a rail of dresses, trying to choose.*

Way of the world, way of the good old bad old world.

POPPY. We can always try to make things better.

She finds an alluring black-and-gold Chinese dress.

TOMMY. Sorry to break it to you, gal, but good intentions don't make a jot of difference...

POPPY. What hope is there for any of us then?

TOMMY. I'd plump for that frock if I was you. Bet you'd look a sight better than I did as Lily Ping-Pong from old Hong Kong.

TOMMY *plays a fragment of a Chinese theme.*

POPPY *reddens and puts back the black-and-gold Chinese dress.*

POPPY. Have you tried looking in the cellar for your sheep?

TOMMY. That cellar's a dank and dastardly bottomless pit. You've not stepped a foot down there, have you?

She pulls out a more modest but pretty, chiffon, flowery dress.

POPPY. Smith does sometimes.

TOMMY. Descend that damned cellar and I'd soon be missing too... like all the lost souls foolhardy enough to venture before.

POPPY *gives her newspaper to* TOMMY.

POPPY. Here's something to cheer you up.

TOMMY. *The Workers' Dreadnought.* Where's the artistry in a title like that?

POPPY. It's not meant to be entertaining.

TOMMY. It's succeeding there.

POPPY. It's very informative, you know.

TOMMY. You northeners don't still believe in the little people, do ya?

POPPY. What you on about?

TOMMY. Written by elfs?

POPPY. East London Federation of Suffragettes, soft-head.

TOMMY. Ah so you do still believe in fairies.

POPPY. You wouldn't say that if you went to their office.

TOMMY. Oooh, they have an office, these elfs, do they?

POPPY. A proper one… hive of activity like you've never seen… All these women being seriously industrious… together… And the things they talk about and ask… The things they know.

TOMMY. Could these elfs tell me where my sheep is then?

POPPY *goes behind a screen and undresses*.

POPPY. And guess what?… Mrs Lloyd introduced me to their leader even… She's from up north too… Sylvia, she is… A Pankhurst to boot… How's that!… Looks like you soft southerners need us to come down to give you all a kick up the backside and teach you lot the meaning of progress.

TOMMY. Road to nowhere.

POPPY. It's worth a read.

TOMMY. How's it worth a whole ha'penny?

POPPY. That's just when it's fresh off press for them can afford. We've been taking the rest round and putting them through people's doors for nowt.

TOMMY. Nowt for the *'Nought*, eh?

POPPY. Wouldn't do you any harm to give it a look over. See how there's people fighting the good fight, not giving up at all…

TOMMY. Who said I was giving up?

POPPY *emerges from behind the screen, dress half-done-up*.

POPPY. Are you reading it or pretending?

POPPY *indicates to* TOMMY *to help her with her dress*.

TOMMY. Excuse me, young lady. I'll read what I choose…
Shame of it!

POPPY. What've you found?

TOMMY. Our boys… enlisted soldiers, if you please!… Forced
to carry on warring… as if enough wasn't enough… in
someone else's bloody mess.

He drops the paper and helps with her dress.

POPPY. Where's this?

TOMMY. Against them what's-it-called…

POPPY. Bolsheviks, you mean.

TOMMY. Somewhere in godawful Russia.

POPPY. That's no mess, that's proper revolution, that is.

TOMMY. Does it never bloody end?

POPPY. It wouldn't happen if women ruled the world.

TOMMY. Who told you that?

POPPY. Read page four and you'll find out.

TOMMY. Some of us have our own pressing matters… notably
sheep… to attend to.

POPPY. We could do with your support, you know… I've
already been spat on today by one fella.

POPPY *disappears behind the screen again.*

TOMMY *starts to put on the shepherdess dress.*

TOMMY. Never any excuse for that sort of behaviour.

POPPY. I told him to keep his bile in his own belly.

TOMMY. Did he stop?

POPPY. He ran off alright.

TOMMY. Good for you.

POPPY. Not before cussing at me like the devil and raising a fist.

TOMMY. Bloody nerve. If I'd've been there… I'd have made damn sure that he begged his pardon… and if he didn't… boof! Goodbye to his rotten teeth… gums… jaw… his whole bloody head till he learns how to use them right!

POPPY. And how would lowering yourself to his level help anyone?

TOMMY. Only trying to defend you, aren't I!

POPPY. Take more than a bit of dribble to put me or any of us off.

TOMMY. Don't tell me it didn't cause you any distress all the same.

POPPY. I'll get over it.

TOMMY. Don't we all, don't we all.

POPPY. Thanks for your concern anyhow.

TOMMY (*sings*).
>   'Oh!… Mary loves her little lamb…
>   Forever on her tail…
>   No matter where our Mary goes…'

(*Speaks.*) So where is it now, eh, Mary?

POPPY. Will you bloody well stop calling me that!

TOMMY. No cause for cursing, madam.

POPPY. Promise me you won't do it again.

TOMMY. Then tell me where that blessed sheep is!

POPPY. If it's gone it's gone and that's that.

POPPY *appears from behind the screen, fully dressed now. She seems uncertain, bashful all of a sudden.*

What do you think?

TOMMY (*presenting himself as a shepherdess*). What do you think?

They stare at each other.

TOMMY *starts to improvise a few bars of a romantic waltz.*

Pretty damn pretty.

POPPY. D'you mean it?

TOMMY. Never ask anyone if they mean a compliment. Cash in your winnings and count yourself lucky.

POPPY. But does it suit at least?

TOMMY (*sings*).
 Of all that stirs in verdant field...
 Of all... from fertile soil that springs...
 Of all the blooms... that sunshine brings...
 Of all... of all... Ah... Of all that summer offers
  brightly...
 Of all that flowers daily... nightly...

POPPY. Would you want to step out with me looking like this?

TOMMY. And me a married lady!

POPPY. Oh I didn't mean...

TOMMY (*sings*).
 Of all that blushes bold and sweetly...

 (*Speaks.*) Wouldn't say no.

POPPY. You really wouldn't mind... I mean, if you were a bachelor?

TOMMY. Those were the days.

POPPY. So I'll do?

TOMMY (*sings*).
 Oh... Poppy...

 (*Speaks.*) Happy now?

POPPY. That's better.

TOMMY (*sings*).
>...Ah Poppy, lovely Poppy
>Mmmm you captivating Poppy
>Hum with me, strum with me, come with me
>O'er meadows and streams.
>
>Oh Poppy, darling Poppy
>Mmmm intoxicating Poppy
>Play with me, sway with me, stay with me
>Girl of my dreams.

(*Speaks*.) Are you going barefoot?

POPPY. Oh, shoes.

POPPY *seeks out some shoes*.

TOMMY. He's an ace lad is George. True mucker.

POPPY. Good laugh too... and thoughtful...

TOMMY. Braver than I am.

POPPY. Is he?

TOMMY. I should say.

POPPY. What'd he do?

TOMMY. Ah... ya know... Rescued a few... Risked himself.

POPPY. Did you see it yourself?

TOMMY. Don't go telling him I said so.

POPPY. I've tried asking him...

TOMMY. As you say, a good laugh. What can beat it? That's what we need, isn't it, a good old laugh.

POPPY. Well, I reckon it's pretty brave of you to go out in front of them mobs you call an audience.

TOMMY. Pretty isn't exactly the word I'd choose, luvvie.

GEORGE *walks in. He is wearing his suit and carrying a box.*

GEORGE. And how are my two favourite ladies, this lovely evening?

POPPY. Oh!

GEORGE. Ready then?

POPPY. Give us a tick…

POPPY *flusters around looking for her shoes and hat and gloves, etc.*

GEORGE. Mr Johns, you're looking very… what's the word… em…

TOMMY. Pastoral. The word is pastoral.

GEORGE. Can't wait to see this one frolicking in the fields.

TOMMY. Ha ha ha.

GEORGE. Nah, I mean it… Not kidding.

TOMMY. Ah. Alright. Very well. Then there's nothing else for it… Mary is going to have to go down… Wish me luck.

TOMMY *takes* GEORGE*'s hand and shakes.*

GEORGE. Where you off to in all your finery?

TOMMY. On a mission… A very ill-advised mission… If I don't come back… send out a search party… and if you still don't find me… make sure that Bessie gets the pink-satin robe.

He salutes and stands to attention.

For King George, Britannia and our glorious Empire!

He marches off.

GEORGE. You stitch me up, Tom. Stitch me up.

POPPY *is pretty much ready.*

POPPY. Sorry to keep you waiting.

GEORGE. Don't be silly.

POPPY. Ready now.

GEORGE. Wait… I've got a little something here that's looking for a home.

He hands her the box.

Take a peep if you like.

POPPY *looks inside the box.*

POPPY. Blimey, is this a…

GEORGE *gets a typewriter out of the box.*

GEORGE. Underwood number five.

POPPY. Now that really is something.

GEORGE *places it on a work top/table.*

GEORGE. And this is called a QWERTY keyboard… See, from the top line, Q… W… E…

POPPY. R… T… Y!

GEORGE. It's a damn useful little beast.

POPPY. How much did it cost?

GEORGE. I know someone who knows someone who knows someone.

POPPY. You mean, it's stolen?

GEORGE. No more than the shirt on my back is! D'you really think I'd bring ill-gotten goods here!

POPPY. I'm sorry… I wasn't sure… you know… with your packages and all the supplies you get hold of… and dealings… and…

GEORGE. Surplus to requirements… No longer needed… That's what I look out for… And there's a lot of it about…

POPPY. Sorry.

GEORGE. What you must think of me.

POPPY. I don't. Not really.

GEORGE. Honest?

POPPY. Honest.

They look at each other keenly.

I'm sure Smith'll be very happy with it.

GEORGE. This requires someone to take it on who can fully appreciate the four-bank keyboard with single shift.

POPPY. And what's this?

GEORGE. That's the frontstroke mechanism… Looks like this is missing a ribbon…

POPPY. I could get one from the *Dreadnought* office.

GEORGE. Ah, so you've got your eye on it, have you?

POPPY. Only… to have use of it, like… If no one else needs it right now.

GEORGE. First come, first served, I reckon.

POPPY. I mean, like you said, useful beast, isn't it.

GEORGE. Important to get up new skills, right?

POPPY. I'd say, these days, it's essential.

GEORGE. Well there you are.

POPPY. Really?

GEORGE. If anyone deserves it, you do.

They gaze at each other keenly.

Still want to go out on the town tonight?

POPPY. You bet.

GEORGE. Come on, then.

POPPY *carefully puts the box over the typewriter.*

POPPY. Thanks, George. Thank you so so much.

POPPY suddenly kisses him on the cheek.

GEORGE. Now now.

POPPY smiles.

GEORGE *smiles.*

They keep looking at each other… until they softly, shyly kiss.

GEORGE *takes her by the hand and whisks her off.*

TOMMY *appears.*

TOMMY. Right then, my friends…

TOMMY clocks that POPPY and GEORGE aren't there.

Ah… Gone too, eh?… Oh well…

TOMMY sits at the piano, plays an intro, then improvises.

(*Sings.*)
    Now what is Miss Muffet without her tuffet
    A cock horse without Banbury Cross?
    And what would Jack Horner without his corner
    Or that Mill without its Floss?

(*Speaks.*) And now even… Mary's lost her little lamb.

(*Sings.*)
    She don't know what to do
    She thought she had it on her tail
    Always there without a fail
    But off she went to Belgium bog
    Still it followed like a dog
    Over tops and under… steel
    The bleedin' thing was close at heel
    Across the wastes and through the wire…
    Baa baa baa… the fiercest fire…
    But odd as strange as odd can be
    Now she's back from o'er the sea…

(*Speaks*.) Anyone seen an animal hereabouts? Woolly thing.
Black eyes. Pink mouth. Makes a sound like... bleating?

(*Sings*.)
> But when she looks behind her
> That little friend is gone
> And what will poor dear Mary do...
> Oh what will poor old Mary do...
> Oh what will this poor Mary do... now that I'm alone?

Echoes of bleating of lost sheep.

As TOMMY *gathers all his costumes together, the 'baas'
crescendo and fade.* TOMMY *leaves with his arms full to
bursting.*

Night deepens.

The melody of TOMMY*'s* POPPY *song plays.*

POPPY *wanders on in a dream of delight, kicks off her
shoes.*

POPPY. Play with me... Sway with me... Stay with me...

She approaches the typewriter with awe and delight.

Each... and every... day... with me...

POPPY *raises a finger and taps a single key on the
typewriter... Then she taps another... Then taps another...*

...and night...

Ukelele plays POPPY*'s theme.*

Typewriter keys stiltingly tap a yet-to-be-found rhythm.

Sewing machines whirr.

Scene Four

Red

Outside the workshop the wind blows and whistles.

Inside, SMITH *is completing a tailcoat by hand.*

SMITH. One thread. Not careless.

> *He snips the final stitch.*

No matter how fine…

> *He places it carefully on a hanger…*

No matter how well-crafted a coffin…

> *He adds it to a rack of other newly made pieces of menswear, all black.*

It will not make anyone wish for death.

> *He stretches.*

But at least the undertakers will put on a fine show.

> *He yawns.*

Enough.

> *He goes to the drawers/shelves where the patterns are kept and pulls out exquisite and detailed drawings of Chinese ceremonial gowns.*

Now then…

> *He finds a quiet spot to sit and peruse.*

Hmmm.

> *He surveys the contents of his workshops, takes out rolls of red silk and satin, carefully lays out the fabrics until they cover the entire floor, like a field of red. He meticulously scrutinises the different shades and textures, then takes up a large pair of tailor's shears…*

> *Sound of* GEORGE *and* POPPY *singing outside the door, an upbeat version of the sentimental classic 'After the Ball is Over'.*

POPPY/GEORGE (*sing*).
　　After the ball is over, after the break of morn
　　After the dancers' leaving, after the stars are gone…

　　SMITH *disappears*.

　　POPPY *and* GEORGE *enter. She is now wearing the black Chinese dress*.

　　He wears a suit, collar loosened.

　　Many a heart is aching if you could read them all…

　　They see the silks and gasp.

　　Whoa!

　　POPPY *slips off her shoes and tiptoes across*.

POPPY (*sings*).
　　Many the hopes that have vanished…

GEORGE (*sings*).
　　After the ball.

　　GEORGE *lifts up his leg to get across too*.

POPPY. Not in those clodhoppers of yours.

GEORGE. Best get back anyhow.

POPPY. Already?

GEORGE. Flies by, doesn't it.

POPPY. Always ends too soon.

GEORGE. I'd be with you round the clock if I had the chance.

POPPY. D'you really mean that?

GEORGE. Isn't it what you want me to say?

POPPY. Might be.

GEORGE. What else d'you want me to say?

POPPY. Don't want you to say it just coz you think I'll like it.

GEORGE. What if what you want me to say is what I mean? How would you like that?

POPPY. A lot.

GEORGE. So tell me and I'll say it.

POPPY. Whatever I like?

GEORGE. Try me.

POPPY. Well, I want you to say I'm the most wonderful girl in the world.

GEORGE. I am the most wonderful girl in the world.

POPPY. George!

GEORGE. You are the most wonderful girl in the world.

POPPY. I think of no one but you.

GEORGE. I do think of no one but you.

POPPY. I want to be with you…

GEORGE. I really want to be with you… round the clock.

POPPY. So do I.

GEORGE. We're good company for each other, aren't we?

POPPY. The best.

GEORGE. To have someone, your own special someone… to love and all… doesn't come to everyone.

POPPY. Do you love me then?

GEORGE. I reckon I do.

POPPY. I reckon too.

GEORGE. You do?

POPPY. Truly.

They take this in, rather amazed.

GEORGE. There we have it.

POPPY. Is that all?

GEORGE. What else?

POPPY. What else might there be?

GEORGE. Well... alright... Let's see... So... How'd you feel about making a proper go of it?

POPPY. A proper go?

GEORGE. What the hell... What about getting wed?

POPPY. Wed?

GEORGE. Husband and wife.

POPPY. You and me?

GEORGE. I reckon I'd make you a pretty good husband.

POPPY. What sort of a wife would I make?

GEORGE. Only one way to find out.

POPPY. The thing is... I've got to know...

GEORGE. Go on.

POPPY. Don't want to pry... it's just Sylvia said...

GEORGE. Sylvia?

POPPY. Sometimes you don't listen, do you? She's the one I'm selling the *Dreadnought* for... and she says that a woman should ask a man who expresses serious intentions towards her, if he's ever had anything to do with another woman.

GEORGE. How much to do?

POPPY. You know...

GEORGE. You mean kissing?

POPPY. For starters.

GEORGE. Cuddling?

POPPY. Canoodling and the like.

GEORGE. How much canoodling?

POPPY. As far as it goes.

GEORGE. And what if the man has had something to do with another?

POPPY. The woman should say no to him.

GEORGE. Even if he promises to be true to her forever after?

POPPY. 'Votes for women, Chastity for men.' That's the creed.

GEORGE. Up until now, I've been a bit of a man's man, Poppy. This is the furthest I've gone with a girl.

POPPY. Promise.

GEORGE. Promise.

POPPY. I'm glad.

GEORGE. So what d'you say?

POPPY. Sylvia isn't wed to any man.

GEORGE. Proper spinster, is she?

POPPY. Not one bit… she's settled with some Italian fella.

GEORGE. What kind of settled?

POPPY. Living in their own home together.

GEORGE. Well, that's not on. I'd want to do right by you, not put you in any compromising situation.

POPPY. That's very decent.

GEORGE. What d'you reckon?

POPPY. Can I think about it?

GEORGE. Take as long as you like.

GEORGE *traces his finger across* POPPY*'s lips*.

You brighten up even the dark of night, my darling Poppy.

GEORGE *plants another kiss tenderly on her mouth and then goes to leave.*

POPPY *swoons slightly.*

Sleep tight.

GEORGE *goes.*

POPPY. Lay me down in the stables!

POPPY *drops down onto the fabrics.*

The POPPY *song music plays.*

She relishes the red silk and satin around her, luxuriating in the cloth, enfolding herself in it, urgently feeling its sensual softness. She sings the tune in 'ahs' and 'ohs'.

(*Sings.*)
   …Mmmm…
   Play with me…
   Sway with me…
   Stay with me…

She carefully removes her dress and, in her underwear, caresses the silk, enjoying it with her bare skin.

SMITH *appears.*

SMITH. What are you doing?

POPPY. Oh heck!

POPPY *covers herself.*

Pardon, I… Pardon.

SMITH. What right do you have!

She awkwardly tries to reach over to her clothes.

POPPY. I'll smooth it out… I'll put it all back…

SMITH. Stop. Be quiet. You've done enough.

POPPY *freezes still.*

POPPY. Could you please pass me…

She reaches out to her underwear and the black dress.

SMITH. That black dress…

POPPY. I'm sorry. It's all crumpled… I'm sorry. I'll…

SMITH. The yu-tsi in the Emperor's court wore black dresses like this.

POPPY. The yu-what?

SMITH. There were scores of them. Emperor's concubines.

POPPY. You let me go out dancing with George dressed like a Chinese woman of the street?

SMITH. They lived in the palace.

SMITH *shows the detailed drawings of Chinese ceremonial gowns.*

See!

POPPY. More concubines?

SMITH. Original patterns. Classic patterns. Fixed at the beginning of the Manchu Dynasty. Always followed. This is the form.

He holds out a particular drawing of an intricate and magnificent gown for her to see.

The dress for the Empress.

POPPY. Is it?

SMITH. There was only one Empress.

POPPY. It's quite something.

SMITH. I was planning to make it at last.

POPPY. For anyone in particular?

SMITH. For its own sake.

POPPY. What d'you mean?

SMITH. For the satisfaction of accomplishing such a significant item... To do it justice... And I admit, for my own sake too.

POPPY. I really didn't mean to mess it up for you... Sorry for being so...

SMITH....disrespectful... self-indulgent.

POPPY. All this... redness... though... pure redness... it's just so... so...

SMITH. Expensive.

POPPY. But I couldn't... I mean, how could anyone resist... or ever want to resist... the touch... the feel of it... the beauty of its... its...

SMITH....quality.

POPPY. And silkiness... and... and...

SMITH....refinement.

POPPY. Don't you ever feel tempted yourself?

SMITH. To do what?

POPPY. To surrender... to... all this gorgeous material?

SMITH. It must be cherished...

POPPY. The way it falls and flows... and takes shape... changes shape... and the way you can make your own shapes with it...

SMITH. Form must be formed with great care.

POPPY. Don't you long to be carefree ever?

SMITH. There is a precise way...

POPPY. Or dream...

SMITH. What?

POPPY. Make your dreams come true... It's like the stuff of dreams... so dreamy...

SMITH. Dreamy?

POPPY. Do you never feel moved simply to dream…?

SMITH. Poppy…

POPPY. Don't you?

SMITH. Wait there.

POPPY. Like this!

He presses a finger to his lips.

SMITH. Sh!

He carefully pulls up a floorboard or two, reaches down into the floor and pulls out a large-ish leather-bound, well-used and well-kept scrapbook/sketchbook.

POPPY. What's that?

SMITH. A selection of… my very own… pure silly self-indulgence…

POPPY. Not more patterns?

SMITH. Not at all… Still many blank pages, see…

POPPY. Oh.

SMITH. So… What if… May I…?

POPPY. May you what?

SMITH. I wonder… May I… sketch you?

POPPY. Why?

SMITH. Before we lose this moment… in which you indulge yourself so… beautifully… passionately… tonight… and in which your… irresistible indulgence… you are right… cannot be resisted.

POPPY *blushes.*

POPPY. I wish I hadn't got so carried away now…

SMITH. *Nit dos iz sheyn, vos iz sheyn, nor dos, vos es gefelt*

POPPY. Silly… ridiculous…

SMITH. You asked me the point of copying clothes so carefully
for people to pretend to be what they're not...

POPPY. So?

SMITH. So... I ask myself... am I only ever to fashion... what
has been fashioned before...?

POPPY. Or what you dare... fashion... create... yourself?

SMITH. Starting with...

POPPY. All this?

SMITH. So may I?

POPPY. Sketch me how?

SMITH. As you are.

POPPY. As I am?

SMITH. Well?

POPPY *lets the material drop.*

POPPY. Like this?

She starts to find confidence rising in her own skin.

He sketches swiftly.

SMITH. Let's see...

He circles her as he sketches, getting different perspectives.

POPPY. *Nit dos iz...?*

SMITH. ...*sheyn*... Beautiful is not what is beautiful...
Beautiful is what you like.

POPPY. What you like or I like?

SMITH. What do you like... What are you... really like?

POPPY. Like?... Like... like this?

POPPY *playfully swirls some fabric, making shapes around
herself.*

Or how... how about... like this?

She tries something else with the fabric.

SMITH. Or like this?

He starts to try out the fabric with her too.

POPPY. Like this?

SMITH. Like this?

POPPY. Like this!... Like this...Like this...

SMITH. Like this!... Like this!... Like this...

He suddenly runs about swiftly and wildly opening all the windows and letting in the wind, which blows the fabrics. He pulls more fabrics off shelves. She joins him with glee. SMITH steps back with his sketchbook, watching intently, as POPPY flows with the wind and releases the fabrics.

And so I dream... I work from you!

Scene Five

Head or Heart

A curtain has appeared across the back half of the workshop.

TOMMY *appears, wearing a big coat and hobnail boots, carrying a bottle of whisky.*

TOMMY. Luscious ladies and portly gentlemen!

He takes a swig, then plays a few grand opening chords on the piano.

(*Posh lady's voice.*) We live in one of the most civilised countries in the world...

He takes another swig.

We have the noblest and greatest institutions within our shores...

GEORGE, *wearing trousers and jacket, appears.*

Bank of England. Seat of finance...

GEORGE. Still at it?

TOMMY. Great universities of Oxford and Cambridge. Seats of learning... nicely rounded seats, the pair of them...

GEORGE pulls out a pack of playing cards. And waves them at TOMMY.

GEORGE. Slip in a few hands?

TOMMY. Later.

GEORGE. How late is later?

TOMMY. In a bit.

GEORGE. How much of a bit?

TOMMY. Until I've got this stupid bitch sorted!

GEORGE. Alright!

TOMMY. Sorry... But I need this bint to be on form...

GEORGE. Try being nice to her then. She might appreciate it.

TOMMY. She's on her way... I can feel it... Be with you... Alright?

He plays something of the tune of Lady Davinia's song, muttering to himself.

GEORGE. What if you give it a rest, stop flogging yourself to death?

TOMMY. Ready to send me to the knacker's yard?

GEORGE. All I'm saying is, how you going to give others the pleasure of your entertainment if you're straining yourself like a constipated bear... (*Sees the whisky.*) Oi, are you sharing that or keeping it all for you?

TOMMY raises the bottle.

TOMMY. Up yours.

He swigs long and deep.

GEORGE. You got any dreams, Tom?

TOMMY *hands him the bottle*.

TOMMY. Here.

GEORGE. I've got so many dreams… like the racing… Other stuff too… Even coming true… Don't know what to do with 'em all.

TOMMY. So much for dreams…

He thrusts a paper into GEORGE*'s hands*.

Never in my whole career has a pig-arse of a reporter called me cheap and… get this, then… brutish!

GEORGE. What does one reporter know?

TOMMY. Two… three… four… reporters.

GEORGE. Four's nothing.

TOMMY. 'Excruciatingly excremental.'

GEORGE. Poo to them.

TOMMY. Ha-de-ha.

GEORGE. Don't mock your number-one fan, sweetheart.

TOMMY. Bet if I set the book of bleedin' Deuteronomy to music, they'd still say I was lowering the tone.

GEORGE. Your punters don't want the Salvation Army.

TOMMY. I have had it with those hack scribblers who blow you out with any thoughtless word from their careless little pencils. Are they putting themselves on the line! Are they hell to damnation. Sitting on their backsides. Watching. Commenting. Letting the rest of us take it. And, knock after knock after knock, on we go, giving out, trying to get on with no reward and no appreciation. On and on. Dying out there with the whole shitting world watching. Dying. Over and over again.

GEORGE. You don't die, Tommy.

TOMMY. Oh no?

GEORGE. I've seen folks come again and again.

TOMMY. Not you so much of late though.

GEORGE. Poppy gets a bit sensitive about you taking her off, Tom.

TOMMY. I don't just take her off, do I? Anyhow, you can still come to see us, George, can't you?

GEORGE. Crack me up, you do. Yeah, I'll find the time.

TOMMY. Hey... want to take a peek behind the curtain... See what Smith's up to?

GEORGE. No way.

TOMMY. He's up all hours behind there, isn't he?

GEORGE. Leave him to it, Tom.

TOMMY. You will come to see us again soon, then?

GEORGE. I will, Tom. I will.

> GEORGE *reaches into his pocket and pulls out two epaulettes with coloured piping and regimental numbers.*

You can have one of these if you like.

TOMMY. Not still hanging onto those old Boches' bits.

GEORGE. Nearly got hit ripping these off.

TOMMY. Idiot.

GEORGE. There's nothing like a shell whistling an inch past your ear and missing.

TOMMY. Thanks, but keep 'em.

GEORGE. These are my lucky epaulettes. You're passing up a chance of good fortune here.

> POPPY *and* SMITH *enter carrying packages of fabrics. She also carries a bundle of books and pamphlets.*

SMITH. Salutations, comrades.

POPPY. Good evening.

They acknowledge him. SMITH *sorts out the contents of the packages.* POPPY *helps.*

GEORGE (*to* POPPY). What d'you fancy doing tonight?

TOMMY. Hey, George, what about those hands and jars.

GEORGE. I thought you was h-otherwise h-occupied.

TOMMY. Have I ever let you down?

POPPY. It's alright. You all go. I could do with practising my typing.

POPPY *starts to undo the string around her books.*

TOMMY. Good girl. You with us, Smith?

SMITH. I am otherwise occupied.

He heads towards the curtain.

TOMMY. Hey, first, will you look me over?

TOMMY *unbuttons the coat to reveal women's chemise, pantaloons and corset.*

GEORGE *wolf-whistles.*

TOMMY *sticks up two fingers at him.*

SMITH. Chop-chop. Over here, madame.

TOMMY *plods over to* SMITH.

Are you sure you want undies?

TOMMY. What else gets any attention?

GEORGE *whistles again.*

SMITH *starts to check* TOMMY's *outfit.*

Where was I?

GEORGE. Seats.

TOMMY (*posh voice*). And last, but most certainly not least, our illustrious seat of government, the Houses of Parliament...

SMITH. Stand tall... Taller...

TOMMY. It is with great honour that I, Lady Davinia Dottypants... accept the most worthy position of Member of this Parliament...

POPPY. Is he taking off Nancy Astor now?

GEORGE. Leave him to it.

TOMMY. All my life I have wanted to enter those great portals...

SMITH. Yes, done.

TOMMY *goes to the piano and tinkers with the tune*.

POPPY. But, George... It means so much, for a woman to become...

GEORGE. Impersonation is the greatest form of flattery, isn't it?

POPPY. Then let him do Lloyd George in his droopy underwear!

TOMMY (*sings*).
A lady is a lady
And that's what I am, quite grand
I've received my education
From the best brains in the land
The dons are oh-so-darling
Always keen to lend a hand
But I'm done with dreaming spires
Now it's time to make my stand.

Oh, I'm going to pass a bill
And believe me, sir, I will
To teach the silly boys who say we're weaker
Backbench, front and side
I will show 'em woman's pride
I'm not here to make the teas, Mr Speaker.

SMITH. Poppy, the red velvet?

POPPY *picks up a package and takes it to him.*

He rips it open and holds the velvet up to her face.

Shleymesdik.

TOMMY. Bless you!

SMITH *sighs deeply.*

POPPY. Something wrong with it?

SMITH. Just because it's perfect, doesn't mean it's right.

SMITH, *shaking his head and muttering to himself, disappears with the velvet behind the curtain.*

GEORGE *looks at* POPPY*'s books and pamphlets.*

TOMMY (*sings*).
    I'm a lady on a mission…
    With ideals raised on high…

GEORGE. 'Childbirth and Mortality'?

POPPY. Hot off the press.

GEORGE. Sounds like fun.

GEORGE *looks at the other books.*

TOMMY (*sings*).
    I'm a lady on a mission
    With ideals raised on high
    My cause is prohibition
    Let us keep our glasses dry
    All you sozzled reprobates
    Can carp and curse and cry
    But someone's got to save your souls…

(*Speaks.*) Excuse me, Minister…! Ouch – who threw that!

(*Sings.*)
    How dare you, sir! Oh my!

TOMMY *continues to tinkle*.

GEORGE. 'Marriage and Love', eh?

POPPY. It's not a romance.

GEORGE. You're taking it very serious.

POPPY. Was it not meant serious, what you asked me?

GEORGE. No, it wasn't not meant not to be serious... I
mean... only, heck, how much reading you planning to do?

POPPY. These are by intelligent, forward-thinking people
who've looked into it properly and know the pitfalls... and
some even have ideas about what can be different...

GEORGE. How different?

TOMMY (*sings*).
Oh, I'm going to pass this bill
And believe me, sirs, I will
To teach you silly boys who say we're weaker
Backbench, front and side I will show you woman's pride
No, I'm not here to make the teas, Mr Speaker.

POPPY. Why don't you choose one to take away and read too?
They make sense, George... They really do...

GEORGE. What if some things don't make sense?

POPPY. I want to do what's for the best... not just for me... for
both of us... and forging the right path for all.

GEORGE. For the best... Yeah... That's right... So, for the
best...

TOMMY (*sings*).
A lady has her standards
And I really must admit
The Commons are too common
I don't like it there one bit
All they do is argue
And sit and stand and...?

GEORGE.... sit?

TOMMY (*sings*).
> If this is how one runs a country
> I'd really rather knit.

POPPY *groans loudly*.

> Now I've truly had my fill
> Of the strain to pass a bill
> There's more virtue in a lady mild and meeker
> Backbench, front or side I will swallow down my pride
> Oh, I'd be glad to make the teas, Mr Speaker.

POPPY. Get off!

GEORGE. Tom… would you mind…?

TOMMY. One lump or two, Chancellor? Would the minister like cream with his scone? Dash of milk for the whips?

GEORGE *laughs*. POPPY *glares*.

(*Speaks*.)
> I'd be pleased to make the teas
> Jam or lemon cheese?
> I'd just love to pour your teas.
> Mr Speaker.

POPPY *tuts*.

> Hold your own, my friend. Hold your own… as the Sergeant-at-Arms told Black Rod.

TOMMY *skips off*.

GEORGE. If you let him annoy you, he'll do it all the more.

POPPY. You don't have to join in.

GEORGE. What's wrong with enjoying myself?

POPPY. Like that!

GEORGE. Hey. Come on… Look… His Lordship's wanting me to go up to his country place this month for one of his jaunts…

POPPY. So I won't see you?

GEORGE. Thing is… you could come too… to visit… if you can get away… and we could go for a top drive out in the lanes… might even get up to thirty-five or forty miles an hour… and have our own picnic… make it a real treat… you know…

POPPY. But when would I find the time off… with my work here and helping with the *Dreadnought* and meetings and…?

GEORGE. Look, if getting wed is not…

POPPY. What d'you mean?

GEORGE. If this hesitating and reading is your way of pulling out… No hard feelings. I want only what's best for you. You see that, don't you? And no need to fear telling me straight. I can rely on you to do that, can't I?

POPPY. Oh, don't take it that way…

GEORGE. I realise that I might not be the right man…

POPPY. It's not you, George.

GEORGE. Well, whatever happens, I love you… love you to bits. Always will.

POPPY. Do you still want to…?

GEORGE. With you. Of course… Although it might be that I'm not really cut out for marriage myself… being a freewheeler… and…

GEORGE *takes her hand, lost for words.*

POPPY. You can tell me… tell me anything, you know.

GEORGE. Some things don't make sense… All you can do is trust your heart, right?

POPPY. I suppose…

GEORGE. Come away… stay with me… in the country.

POPPY. I'll see what I can do.

TOMMY *appears, dressed in trousers and shirt, ostentatiously carrying a teapot. He performs to* POPPY *and* GEORGE.

TOMMY. Ready, lads?

GEORGE. Are we off, Tom?

SMITH *appears, looking out of sorts, from behind his curtain.*

TOMMY. Alright, Smith?

SMITH. On second thoughts, a tipple or two would not go amiss.

TOMMY. What's happened to your 'h-otherwise h-occupation'?

SMITH. Of all the manifold and variable alternatives… right now, running away is by far the most appealing.

GEORGE *plants a kiss on* POPPY's *cheek.*

GEORGE. Happy typing.

TOMMY. Royal Duchess or Three Butchers?

SMITH. What's wrong with both?

TOMMY, GEORGE *and* SMITH *leave.*

POPPY *sets up her typewriter, opens one of her books and concentrates.*

POPPY (*reading as she types*). 'The popular notion about marriage and love is that they cover the same human needs…'

She pauses again and looks dreamily into space.

'I only want what's best for you.'

She sighs… then reads.

'Yet the worlds of man and woman are so different from one another… comma… that in truth they remain forever strangers… full stop.'

She pauses thoughtfully.

What about Mr and Mrs Lloyd... The affectionate way they are together... And Mam and Dad know what the other's thinking half the time...?

She reads.

'Marriage is primarily an economic arrangement invented by men... full stop... Women as property... hyphen... sexual and reproductive slaves... exclamation mark!'

But what if you're offered a treasure trove... the most precious thing you've ever found? 'Dante's motto over *Inferno* applies with equal force to marriage: "Ye who enter here leave all hope behind."' What if you want to hope? What if you want to trust? What about throwing in your lot with the one who holds your hand and makes you twice the person you are? What if you feel stronger and brighter and like you could do anything in the world with him at your side? And the pair of you together could take turns in leading the way. And he can freewheel and I can stride forth. What if we can make a marriage in our own way, between us, rather than be made according to some way it's meant to be?

'Love you to bits. Always will.' And so do I. I do. I do I do.

And I will tell you so. I will, George. Yes, I'll tell you.

She shuts the book and picks up another, opens it, focuses, starts to type again with more determination than ever.

Sounds of typing finding its rhythm as POPPY *continues to bash away.*

Times passes. Light fades.

Music of darkening night.

POPPY *starts to flag and takes herself off to bed.*

The workshop dims and hushes.

Rustling somewhere outside.

Two figures stumble in, breathing heavily.

SMITH *lights a lamp and its glow reveals that* GEORGE *is with him, shirt covered in blood. They speak in hushed voices.*

SMITH. Did anyone follow us?

GEORGE. They'd likely be here by now if they had.

SMITH *and* GEORGE *listen keenly.*

Remind me to keep out of it next time.

SMITH. I reminded you this time.

GEORGE. How could I leave that Indian fella down like that?

SMITH. He didn't seem to appreciate the help.

GEORGE. He damn well should've kept his mouth shut instead of facing them old sailor boys off…

SMITH. They wouldn't have given him a chance either way…

GEORGE. Damn lucky they bolted when the police whistles blew…

SMITH. He got off lightly… because of you… should be grateful… And you should be wiser!

GEORGE. How much bleedin' blood can a person have up their nose! This is my new shirt!

SMITH. Let me see to it.

GEORGE *unbuttons his shirt, takes it off, gives it to* SMITH.

Underneath the shirt, GEORGE *is wearing bandages tightly bound around the chest. The blood has seeped through to these too.*

GEORGE. I'll be alright now.

SMITH. Stay here tonight, in the back room.

GEORGE *nods.*

SMITH *leaves with the bloody shirt.*

Now all alone, GEORGE *examines the blood staining the bandages and slowly, carefully removes the bandages, bit by little bit… to reveal a bare chest and breasts.* GEORGE *is a woman.*

S/he stretches out arms and upper body, feeling the space, breathes in and out deeply with a sigh, then gathers the bloody bandages and goes.

From the shadows, POPPY *emerges, uncertain, confused. She goes to follow* GEORGE, *then turns back and retreats to her room.*

The workshop descends into deep, silent darkness.

Scene Six

Close Shave

Dawn rises.

TOMMY *is sitting at the piano, silent, still as still.*

As rays of light fall into the workshop, he plays a single note, then another, then another. He plays just for himself, to himself, improvising, part-singing, part-speaking. No one else is there.

TOMMY.
> They said there's a silver lining…
> Through the dark cloud shining…
> They said to turn it inside out…
> Well tell me… what were they on about?
>
> They said that once we're homeward bound
> The mire would dry where once we drowned
> We'd find our long sought field of green…
> But tell me… what if some other Joe's been ploughing it,
>   stripped it clean, eh?

> They said the love was waiting…
> Beyond the heart that's breaking…
> They said the home fires never died…
> They said a lot of things, didn't they?

Home fires melody plays, sad and lost.

And me, what do I say?

I say…

> Spin on
> Ride the merry-go-round
> Roll the dice, turn the wheel
> Play the cards whatever they deal
> Spin on, spin on
> With the winds as they blow
> Wherever they throw me, mow me, go wherever they
> Hurl me whirl me twirl me swirl me
> Send me bend me rend me in a
> No-never-ending dance
> So what if I leave the rest… leave it all to… chance?

Morning light is strong now.

POPPY *appears*.

POPPY. Where did you come from?

TOMMY. Is this an angel I see? Have I died and gone to heaven?

POPPY. What happened last night?

TOMMY. You don't want to know.

POPPY. Please tell me.

TOMMY. I rolled in worse for wear and Bessie's not happy. And I'm not happy at the way she's not happy, not at all happy and I made myself very clear about just how unhappy I was and she accuses me of blaming her and I blame her for accusing me and then I tells her to shut it or else… 'Or else what?' she's mewling… And I'm, 'Or else, you'll see, OR ELSE!' And she starts with her weeping… That's what she

does she weeps and wails and says how she can't bear it any
more and how it was easier without me and how she wishes
that I'd never come back and that's the truth the plain truth
and there's other men who'd treat her proper and kindly and
I asks her what man and this time she doesn't deny it. That
man. Well, let him have her. They're welcome to each other.

POPPY. Oh.

TOMMY. So it goes.

POPPY. But what happened before you went home?

TOMMY. Was there a before?

POPPY. When you were out with Smith and… George.

TOMMY. There was some trouble. I got well away from it.
George went towards it. Trust George. Smith went after him.

POPPY. Is there anything you want to tell me about George?

TOMMY. What kind of anything?

POPPY. Anything a girl ought to know about her beau?

TOMMY. Not that I haven't said already.

POPPY. Nothing?

TOMMY. Don't think so.

POPPY. Honestly?

TOMMY. Why?

SMITH *appears carrying a towel over his arm, jug of water,*
bowl, soap.

SMITH. Good morning.

TOMMY. If you say so.

SMITH. We may as well try.

TOMMY. Try dying?

SMITH/TOMMY. Or die trying.

SMITH. Freshen up, my friend.

SMITH *gives the bowl, etc., to* TOMMY.

TOMMY.
> They say that when you're mucky
> All you need is slosh and soap
> A scrub, a rub and good as new…

GEORGE *enters, wearing clean trousers, shirt, waistcoat.*
He carries another towel, tray with shaving soap, brush,
razor, sharpening leather.

For where there's soap there's…

GEORGE.…hope?

POPPY. Are you alright this morning, George?

GEORGE. Well enough.

POPPY. I heard there was some trouble last night.

GEORGE. Near-miss… but we got out of it.

SMITH *disappears behind the curtain.*

POPPY. How about I help you with your shave?

GEORGE. This is for Tommy.

TOMMY. Ta but a wash'll do me.

He washes himself very carefully and thoroughly bit by
little bit.

POPPY. Let me do it for you, George.

GEORGE. I've just had a wash.

POPPY. Please let me.

GEORGE. Don't much like other people shaving me.

POPPY. Don't you trust me?

GEORGE. D'you know how?

POPPY. Used to cut my cousins' hair and shave them same time
once they got bigger… When did you start to need to shave,
George?

GEORGE. About fifteen, sixteen something.

POPPY. Does that sound about right to you, Tommy?

TOMMY. Why wouldn't it?

POPPY. Go on. Sit down.

POPPY *places a chair by the shaving stuff.*

GEORGE. You sure you know how.

POPPY. I can raze a face smooth as my own.

GEORGE. But I'd prefer...

POPPY. And maybe we can have a little word.

TOMMY. Leave you to it.

POPPY. No need to go, Tom.

TOMMY. Good luck, my friend.

TOMMY *nips off.*

GEORGE. Is something amiss this morning?

POPPY. What if I was to say yes.

GEORGE. So there is something amiss?

POPPY. To your proposal.

GEORGE. You're accepting?

POPPY. Didn't you say last night about trusting my heart?

GEORGE. I did.

POPPY. Well, I read and I thought and I realised I felt... I truly felt... ready to overcome my principles and qualms... to promise myself to you... Decided you really were the man for me... So are you happy now I've said yes?

GEORGE. If you're happy, I'm happy, love.

GEORGE *sits.*

She puts a towel round his shoulder.

POPPY. Is this how you imagine married life, George?

POPPY *picks up the soap dish, pours water and starts to lather.*

GEORGE. What, here, like this?

POPPY. I mean, getting up together every morning…

She lathers his face.

Just the two of us in our own cosy little home wherever that might be…

POPPY *sharpens the razor on the leather.*

…before you go off to your motors… with me taking care of you the best way I can… Is this how you want it?

POPPY *raises the razor.*

And what if I was to shave you every single day…?

POPPY *approaches* GEORGE *to start to shave.*

GEORGE. Careful.

POPPY *suddenly stops.*

POPPY. Why am I pretending…?

GEORGE. I told you I prefer to see to it myself.

GEORGE *wipes his face clean with the towel.*

POPPY. Why are you pretending…?

GEORGE. Just act normal, will you…

POPPY. Act normal? Like you…?

GEORGE. Like yourself…

POPPY. I saw the bloody bandages come off.

Silence.

In here. I saw everything. I saw…

GEORGE. Sh!

POPPY. Oh, don't you want anyone to hear… (*Louder.*) that there's not a spot of stubble on your face? Why is that, George?

GEORGE. Sh now.

POPPY. Why the hell did you ask me to marry you…?

GEORGE. Couldn't stop myself… out it popped… and it felt good too… Didn't it… felt right… didn't it?

POPPY. Right? How does that make sense?

GEORGE. I told you, didn't I – some things don't make sense…

POPPY. Were you going to go through with it…?

GEORGE. I was going… to try… to find the right moment…

POPPY. How far were you going to go…?

GEORGE. To see if you'd understand… I thought you might… because…

POPPY. You think me a silly little sap!

GEORGE.…because I've never met a woman like you before.

POPPY (*loud*). I've sure as heck never met one like you!

GEORGE. Sh. Don't.

POPPY. You should not have let me fall in so deep.

GEORGE. I fell too.

POPPY. You were in the driving seat.

GEORGE. Was I?

TOMMY, *dressed in shirt and trousers, appears, carrying a bag.*

TOMMY. You know, on consideration, this morning might not be so very bad after all. Not only am I an eligible bachelor once again… of sorts… but guess what, George?

GEORGE. Have you found something, Tom?

TOMMY. As it happens, I have found an old flame who I thought was gone for good... My own, yes, my dear angel... And I wasn't half fond of her...

POPPY. Amazing what you can discover when you open your eyes and look properly, isn't it, George?

GEORGE. Come on, Pop... Hey...

POPPY. I mean really look, you see... Really notice... I mean, don't you think you ought to come clean, George?

TOMMY. Have you been a naughty boy, George?

POPPY. What kind of naughty have you been, George... And what are you going to do to put it right?

GEORGE. Please... Leave it... Just leave it...

POPPY. A naughty what, George... Well? Because it's not exactly a naughty boy, now, is it, that you have been... and are still being, tell the truth... So what is it? What is it, exactly that you have been... that you are... Well?!... Go on!... Go on then...!

SMITH (*off. Behind the curtain*). Ai-ai-ai! Give me some peace!

SMITH *suddenly emerges from behind the curtain*.

See these ears! They've had enough of your noise!

POPPY. But...

SMITH. Enough, I said... And see these hands! They've also had enough... more than enough... Idiotic hands! Ach!... My master used to rap these hands with a piece of cane. And he was right to do it... Discipline and craft is all!... What a presumptuous dupe I've been... allowing myself to be waylaid... no... seduced... What a frail fool... as ever as ever as ever... not again... and just... listen to you!

POPPY. You're accusing me!

SMITH. Who else distracted me! Diverted into believing that I know better... better than the methods, tried, tested, meticulously practiced, of generations! *Luftmensch!* Without the correct way, what is there? A thing that has no form... worthless nonsense... worse... a thing come from sheer indulgence... and intoxication... a thing that... no matter how perfect... how beautiful the velvet, the silk... comes to nothing... but an unholy mess... the waste of it! Show some respect and keep your *mishegas* to yourself at least... petty personal nonsense...

POPPY. How can you say that to me!

SMITH. *Gornisht*, Poppy. *Drek*.

Silence.

GEORGE. What you got in the bag, Tommy?

TOMMY. Long-lost treasures, my friend.

GEORGE. Anyone special to show us?

TOMMY. She's been resting a while.

GEORGE. How about letting her out?

TOMMY. Maybe another time...

GEORGE. No time like the present.

TOMMY. Only I s'pose I'd better be searching for lodgings ...

GEORGE. That can wait... Let her out.

TOMMY. Is she wanted?

GEORGE. Right now, more wanted than anything, mate.

TOMMY. Smith?

SMITH *sighs.*

SMITH. Why not.

TOMMY. Ah well... Once, in her heyday, she was quite the glittering shimmering presence of divine perfection come down to earth...

He pulls a ballerina's tutu with little fairy wings out of the bag.

Please welcome, Leonora… my first, my very first darling
girl. Here I began. Imagine her, dear friends, fresh, new
gorgeous… in the beginning… Her Coppelia – what a doll…
As Odette – what a swan… And her Plum Fairy, pure sugar.

GEORGE *smiles*. POPPY *and* SMITH *are silent*.

(*Sings in a soft, refined voice.*)
    I was born in a trunk, by the side of the stage
    Mum was a fairy and Dad was a page
    While the corps was a-leaping and jumping about
    I suddenly knew it was time to come out
    I pushed and I pushed, as they pounded the boards
    I pushed and I pushed, it was all major chords
    But no matter how hard I tried on that day
    There was something constricting got right in the way…

    'Is it me?' said me mum
    'No it's it,' said me dad
    'Are you sure?' said me mum.
    'Yes, I'm right.'
    'It's not me.' I did cry
    'And I'm telling you why.
    It's you coz your tights is too tight.'

GEORGE *claps*. SMITH *can't help but smile*.

    From the second I stood I just wanted to dance
    I watched every show, I was all in a trance
    So I knocked on the door of the grandmaster's class
    I said if you train me, I know that I'll pass.
    And he taught me of all the positions to do
    Legs under and over, hands up and through
    But no matter how hard, and I really did try
    Not one of my partners could lift me on high.

    'Is it me?' said the one
    'No it's her,' said the next
    'Are you sure?' said the first
    'Yes, I'm right.'
    'It's not me.' I did cry
    'And I'm telling you why.
    It's you coz your tights is too tight.'

Now I'm top of the pile, the best there can be
Prima ballerina they love to call me
The model of elegance, beauty and grace
Expressive of attitude, arms, feet and face
I have my admirers, the flowers they throw
And the queues at my door do nothing but grow
Great lords lay themselves prostrate at my feet
All in search of my favours, they plead and entreat.

'Is it me?' begs the Duke
'No it's me,' longs the Earl
'Please have me,' prays the Prince
'How they fight.'
'No can do.' I do cry
'And I'm telling you why.
There's no room coz me tights is too tight.'

TOMMY *sings in his own voice.*

No can do, I do cry
And I'm telling you why
There's no room any more
There's no way, what's it for
No can do, coz...

(*Speaks*.) Not only Leonora...

But all my old darlings...

He acknowledges SMITH, *and extracts the odd prop from the bag...*

(*Speaks*).

Nervous Nellie, twitches and tics
Juicy Lucy, grapes by the bunch
Sonia the Sleepwalker, zzzzz
Tessa the human trumpet, ba-da
Spoilt little Trixie-Belle, wah-wah-wah
Even Flighty Aphrodite, ahhhh...

He withdraws a pink-satin robe out of the bag.

Beautiful bit of satin this... Oh well, never mind...

He wistfully tosses it away.

(*Sings*.)
> No can do…
> Yes I'm through…
> Coz their tights is too too too…

(*Speaks*.) Loosen up, my friends. Live a little! Spread your wings… and… Whoooosh… Wish me luck…

TOMMY *leaps off and out into the world.*

SMITH *starts to look around the workshop, sizing up what's there.*

SMITH. And now?… What now…?

SMITH *starts to explore items and materials in the workshop, considering each one with care.*

POPPY. When did you know about George?

SMITH. Since the moment I laid eyes upon him.

POPPY. From the very first?

SMITH. I see people, you see.

POPPY. Why didn't you tell me?

SMITH. If you didn't see, Poppy, you didn't see.

POPPY. But you could have…?

SMITH. Well, now you do see, yes?

POPPY. Now, I do…

SMITH. There you are.

POPPY. But no thanks to…

SMITH. And now… Ah… Now, let's look beyond… let's look afresh… How about…?

SMITH *takes up some green satin, a pot of what sounds like beads and tailor's shears.*

Yes… Again let's see… and leap?

SMITH *vanishes behind the curtain.*

POPPY *goes to her typewriter, opens a book and resumes her practising.*

GEORGE. You're improving.

POPPY *ignores* GEORGE *and types.*

Didn't you say you decided to trust your heart?

POPPY. More fool me.

GEORGE. If you're going to be a fool for anything, best be a fool for love, hey?

GEORGE *takes her hand.*

POPPY. What are you doing?

GEORGE. Do you still care for me?

POPPY. What?

GEORGE. I'm still the person I was last night, the one you decided for.

POPPY. Not to me, you're not.

GEORGE. Let me make it up to you.

POPPY. How can you even begin.

GEORGE. Ask me something. Go on. Ask me. Anything you like.

POPPY. What's your real name?

GEORGE. George Sampson.

POPPY. Tell me the truth for once!

GEORGE. I do drive autos, I did work as a doorman for a while, I was in the war...

POPPY. Playing the hero?

GEORGE. Doing my bit before it ended.

POPPY. What else did you do that you didn't tell me?

GEORGE. Plaited my sisters' hair... like you did.

POPPY. Where are they now, your sisters?

GEORGE. In cages.

POPPY. And you're not?

GEORGE. Not any more.

POPPY. Lies wrap around a person like chains.

GEORGE. How have I been lying?

POPPY. Hiding such a secret!

GEORGE. Everyone hides secrets, don't they?

POPPY. There's secrets and… secrets!

GEORGE. So now you're getting to know me better.

POPPY. Do I want to?

GEORGE. D'you think you could?

POPPY. Did your cage have a husband in it?

GEORGE. And children.

POPPY. D'you ever see them?

GEORGE. Not any more.

POPPY. Don't you want to?

GEORGE. Better this way.

POPPY. Where are they?

GEORGE. They needed a good home.

POPPY. Do they have one now?

GEORGE. Sisters help each other in all sorts of ways.

POPPY. That must be hard for you.

GEORGE. It's easier, as it goes.

POPPY. D'you mean that?

GEORGE. I do, yes.

POPPY. And your husband?

GEORGE. He went missing in Belgium.

POPPY. Did you love him?

GEORGE. Peas in a pod since we were nippers… Always in it together… Couldn't be left behind like that… first him determined to join up… Would've joined him if I could've… and then he goes and goes missing… That was it… What was I meant to do, sit around and wait… Wait for what… the rest of my life?… So I got myself a uniform… like he had done… I went to search…

POPPY. Did you find him?

GEORGE. Not much left when they did. So then I did know for sure… And I should've gone back after that. But I couldn't… And not just because what was there back home now without him?… But… No going back, see… Not after taking off… Not after pulling it off… Boy, that was something… because I was finding… finding… what I hadn't realised I was looking for… someone else… someone who stuck with me… And here he was… full of life and raring to go… How could he go missing too?… No way. George Sampson… was here to stay.

POPPY. And he lets you go places and do what you like, does he?

GEORGE. Never got such chances before. Only one way to go, see, and that's forwards.

POPPY. Look again, Smith said, didn't he?

GEORGE. So let's still go dancing.

POPPY. How can I?

GEORGE. Put one step in front of the other.

POPPY *types*.

They say you only know who you're best suited to when you've danced with them.

POPPY. Is that what they say?

GEORGE. D'you really want us never to dance together ever again?

POPPY. I wish I didn't.

GEORGE. So you do want to?

POPPY *types*.

Give us a chance.

POPPY *suddenly stops typing*.

POPPY. Well, how about…?

GEORGE. Go on.

POPPY *goes to some dresses that are hanging*.

POPPY. How about… one of these?

GEORGE. Whatever you want to wear I'm happy.

POPPY. For you.

GEORGE. Are you kidding?

POPPY. Start again. Properly.

GEORGE. Can't we take it from where we are?

POPPY. Consider it at least?

GEORGE. That's just daft, suggesting that.

POPPY. Oh is it!

GEORGE. Come on… just ridiculous… you know what I mean…

POPPY. I'm not sure I want to know any more about what you mean, George.

POPPY *clears up the props, bag and pink-satin robe that* TOMMY *has left strewn*.

Now, if you don't mind, I need to get on.

GEORGE. Yeah, well, I've got things to attend to too, you know.

GEORGE *leaves*.

Sound of car engine revving.

POPPY *returns to her typing.*

Behind the curtain, the silhouette of SMITH *beavers away.*

Sound of typewriters and sewing machines throbbing with increasing vigour and speed.

Scene Seven

Seeds

The workshop becomes a clear space but for the curtain still hanging towards the back.

TOMMY, *dressed in a suit and coat, appears.*

TOMMY. My lords, ladies, mongrels and elfs, 'Who's the bloke in the coat?' you're asking. Who indeed?

Some confused punter who's wandered through the stage door by mishap? The bailiff after that shady pair keeping low on the fifth row? Gotcha!... Relax, it's just an old mate of yours who's had enough of bleating that he's lost his sheep and is now off to frolic in pastures new. But before I scamper away, I hope you'll give me the grace to share a few passing thoughts:

What d'you get if you cross a pig with a zebra?
Striped sausages.

What d'you get if you cross a priest with temptation?
Cardinal sin.

What d'you get if you cross a soldier with his underwear?
Yes, you've got it. Tommy Johns!

POPPY *appears, dressed in the pink-satin robe, heading towards her room.*

And here's the lady herself… rather resplendent, I see.

POPPY. Hope you don't mind me wearing this about the place. It's so comfy.

TOMMY. Honestly, have you asked the Goddess of Love if she minds her fine apparel being given domestic use backstage?

POPPY. Waste not want not.

TOMMY. Oh well, even so, you're pulling her off far better than I ever did. Look at you. How's a boy to compete.

POPPY. All set for tomorrow?

TOMMY. Southampton here I come-diddly-come.

POPPY. Quite a voyage ahead.

TOMMY. Likely spend it spewing my guts to the fishes.

POPPY. What about your sea legs?

TOMMY. Ran off with that blessed sheep.

POPPY. Will you tread the boards in New York too?

TOMMY. Who knows.

POPPY. How will you make your way?

TOMMY. With what Smith calls chutzpah, I guess. And how are you getting on, divine mistress?

POPPY. Up to eighty words per minute with barely any mistakes… Finished my first bit of reporting for the *Dreadnought*… and they want me to do some more.

TOMMY. George has been missing you.

POPPY. What did he say?

TOMMY. He didn't have to.

POPPY. Well…

TOMMY. He's been a darn sight glummer about the lack of his good lady than I have about that madame who once passed as my 'faithful' wife, damn her to hell, spit on her name, et cetera.

POPPY. What about your children?

TOMMY. I'll send what I can for them.

POPPY. Won't you miss them?

TOMMY. They had trouble recognising me when I came back from the front anyhow. Never settled since. So it goes.

POPPY. Did George say anything else to you?

TOMMY. Apart from how he got up to forty-five miles per hour and how to win races, not much. Hey, can't you just give him another chance? Whatever he's done, can't be so bad that a true heart won't mend it.

POPPY. Well, you see...

SMITH *appears*.

SMITH. Do I hear the voice of the new Columbus?

TOMMY. Pilgrim Father, at your service.

SMITH. You know, I was on my way to the New World when I landed here.

POPPY. Why stop in this old midden?

SMITH. For what else? A lady.

TOMMY. Nothing like love to throw you off-track.

SMITH. And was that anything like love.

TOMMY. Pray to old Neptune that he doesn't take me down.

SMITH. My dear friend...

TOMMY. I don't know how to say...

SMITH. Let us walk up the street and through the market one last time...

TOMMY. Maybe a little detour on the way?

SMITH. A tot of rum to bring out the sailor in you?

TOMMY. You know, that might just help.

SMITH. *Wan shi kai tou nan.*

TOMMY. Is that so?

SMITH. All things are difficult before they are easy.

TOMMY. Fare thee well, Poppy. And whenever you wear that robe, please remember the sorry soldier in skirts for a smiling moment, and most important of all, remember to be your most divine self.

POPPY. Thank you kindly, and safe journey.

> TOMMY *blows her a kiss and sweeps out of the workshop.*

> SMITH *leaves too.*

> POPPY *steps towards her room.*

> They've gone.

GEORGE (*off*). Give me a bit longer.

POPPY. You can't spend the rest of your life in there.

GEORGE (*off*). Who says.

POPPY. Come out.

> GEORGE *reluctantly appears, dressed in a dress.*

> Hello.

> POPPY *holds out her hand.*

> Mary Louisa Wright... but I prefer to be called Poppy.

> GEORGE *takes her hand and shakes it.*

GEORGE. Ruby Morgan... but you can call me George.

POPPY/GEORGE. Pleased to meet you.

They look at each other as if for the first time.

POPPY. You could have come out in your true colours to say goodbye to Tommy.

GEORGE. I'll be seeing him… driving him tomorrow for his train. First thing.

POPPY. Will you let him know then?

GEORGE. What's the point?

POPPY. Isn't he your friend?

GEORGE. Exactly.

POPPY. But if he's your real friend…

GEORGE. He'll have enough on his mind without me bothering him.

POPPY. I bet he'd be chuffed to see you like this.

GEORGE. Oh, a source of amusement, am I?

POPPY. You look a different shape, you know.

GEORGE (*imitating* TOMMY). 'It's not me coz me tights is too tight.'

They both smile.

Missed you.

POPPY. Me too.

GEORGE. Not the same, dancing with anyone else.

POPPY. So you've been out dancing?

GEORGE. Only once.

POPPY. Did you meet anyone?

GEORGE. Not especially.

POPPY. Promise.

GEORGE. Like I said, not the same dancing with anyone else.

POPPY (*sings*).
>   After the ball is over…

She starts to sway and dance a little.

>   After the break of morn…

GEORGE (*sings*).
>   After the dancers' leaving…

POPPY/GEORGE (*sing*).
>   After the stars are gone…

>   GEORGE *opens her arms to invite* POPPY *to dance.*

>   Many a heart is aching…

>   POPPY *enters the dance hold.*

>   If you could read them all…

>   POPPY *and* GEORGE *waltz together.* GEORGE *leads.*

Music plays in accompaniment.

>   Many the hopes that have vanished…
>   After the ball.

Music of the song plays as they continue to dance.

POPPY. This reminds me of school.

GEORGE. Can't see the connection myself.

POPPY. After hours. Miss Pembridge would put on her gramophone…

GEORGE. Oooh, Miss Pembridge had a gramophone, did she!

POPPY. There was a group of us… Did you never have a waltz with your best friend?

GEORGE. There was a gang of us.

POPPY. Who was the leader?

GEORGE. My brother Johnnie.

POPPY. Did you really have four brothers, three sisters…?

GEORGE.... and only one bicycle between the lot of us. Yep.

POPPY. What's Johnnie doing now?

GEORGE. Scarlet fever got him. Way back.

POPPY. I'm sorry.

GEORGE. Thirteen months older he was, always three inches taller.

> POPPY *strokes* GEORGE*'s cheek.*

POPPY. Do you like that?

GEORGE. I dunno really.

> POPPY *strokes* GEORGE*'s neck.*

POPPY. What about that?

GEORGE. Couldn't say.

> POPPY *strokes the back of* GEORGE*'s neck and kisses her hands.*

POPPY. Didn't realise you could carry on doing dancing and all... with your best friend when you grew up. Thought it was just practice before the real thing with your husband.

GEORGE. Best friends, hey?

POPPY. You've got a lovely face.

GEORGE. What makes you say that?

POPPY. I suddenly noticed it all over again.

GEORGE. Don't look too close now.

POPPY. Why can't you be soft?

GEORGE. I'm not made that way.

POPPY. Try letting yourself.

> POPPY *kisses* GEORGE *gently on the cheek.*
>
> Hello.

GEORGE. Hello.

They kiss.

Let's still make a proper go of it.

POPPY. What kind of go?

GEORGE. Why not get wed?

POPPY. How could we?

GEORGE. Like we were going to in the first place... like you said you decided... and to the world we'd be man and wife... and behind closed doors we can... be whatever we choose... Like this even... now and then... if you really want.

POPPY. But, Ruby...

GEORGE. Only... please don't call me...

POPPY. Why not?

GEORGE. Because you make me feel more like George than anyone ever.

POPPY. But that's not what I mean to do...

GEORGE. You're my better half, see...

POPPY. There's so much still to find out...

GEORGE. Marry me...

POPPY. We don't have to keep on playing that old game...

GEORGE. We could make it work our way... the way we want it to work...

POPPY. There's no need to pretend any more, Ruby.

GEORGE *pulls away.*

GEORGE. All I want is to have free rein.

POPPY. So be who you really are.

GEORGE. I told you, George Sampson is who I am.

POPPY. You don't need him to get you anywhere... not really... not anywhere that matters...

GEORGE. How else do I get a job as a chauffeur, at a jolly decent wage with excellent perks and working conditions?

POPPY. I'm ready to fight to my dying breath to get every woman true equality with any man in this land.

GEORGE. It didn't happen in the last ten thousand years so why should it now?

POPPY. Work alongside me... Join with our other sisters... Raise up your life as an example with your skills and know-how, showing the new way, giving others a leg-up, by living openly, freely, truly.

GEORGE. Poppy, love, you can't make anyone else's way for them.

POPPY. We're in it together, aren't we?

GEORGE. All I want to do is drive cars...

POPPY. No one's stopping you.

GEORGE. Not now they're not.

POPPY. What kind of freedom is that, to be George who drives roughshod over the bowed backs of the rest of womankind?

GEORGE. Well, excuse me, but here's one who's stopped bowing... who's stepped up and out... who gives thanks every day for no longer being held in while the greatest show on earth's going on out there... No more tied up in tangles by apron strings that I'd always been taught to knot myself into without even a question... playing a part that I thought was the way of it until... the only one that made it bearable did his disappearing act... And anyhow why did it all have to depend on him...?

POPPY. That's precisely...

GEORGE. And you know one thing that makes my day... To be invited to throw a ball around... being welcome in the game... and kicking with the best of them... playing a few hands… And it might not be lofty and important… but it tickles me pink… Here's one who's on my way. And I tell you this, it's the road for me. And if you can't see… if you just want to make me do it your way… if you can't cheer me on instead of trying to pull me back… what kind of love is that? So… so… Excuse me.

GEORGE *disappears back to* POPPY's *room.*

POPPY *calls after* GEORGE.

POPPY. I'm sorry… I didn't mean… Ruby… I mean… George… I understand… I do… It's the same for me… We're like each other… We are… more than you realise… Of course, you don't have to do anything you don't want… That's not what I meant… But, George… think of where you got him… born from the sodden mud when you went to look for your husband… And that was brave and daring and how many would have the guts to go all the way there? But then he stuck to you… And you feel safe inside him… I see that… But can't you see how he's holding you back now? Clean yourself. Wash him off. You don't need him to protect you any more… I'm going to… I'm coming on in… We can not put on anything… be in our own skins… I want to be with you just as you are… I want you to be with me as I am too… and let's know each other… really know each other… without anything… nothing in the way…

GEORGE *appears, dressed in chauffeur uniform.*

Did you hear me just then?

GEORGE. Pretty much.

POPPY. So?

GEORGE. Best get back… One of the engines is playing up.

POPPY. Please… give yourself… give me… give us… a proper chance.

GEORGE. Haven't we done that?

POPPY. What about loving me to bits and always will?

GEORGE. What about it?

POPPY. Well I...

GEORGE. Don't...

POPPY. Let me say it at least.

GEORGE. Please don't tell me that you love me for who I really am.

POPPY. I do.

GEORGE. Who you think I am isn't who I am.

POPPY. It's only hard at first... to open up to each other, see... It'll get easier... for both of us... if we really try...

GEORGE. Not a word, right. Don't let on, not to a living soul...

POPPY. But...

GEORGE. Promise me. Not a word.

POPPY. I would never say anything to harm you...

GEORGE. Promise.

POPPY. Why d'you want to be a man anyway? You think they don't suffer for their so-called freedom and power? Look at the cost to each one. See what they give up... how many, how much has been lost.

GEORGE. We'll not bother each other again. I'll be off. And I'll keep away from here.

POPPY. George...

GEORGE. I'll be following the Spirit of Ecstasy wherever she leads... at the hub of the wheels as they spin... never stuck in the ruts... She's my mascot... She's the woman of the future and I'm her champion... How far forwards can we go... fast and free as the wind... Even sound has a speed, you know... imagine driving... flying... faster than the speed of sound... And I'm going to race. I'll make it to Monte Carlo. I will. For starters... If any time's the time to go for what drives you deep down... If it isn't now, when is it?

POPPY. Ruby…

> GEORGE *starts to leave*.

GEORGE. Look after yourself, Mary. That's your real name, isn't it? Best live by who you really are, eh?

POPPY. Is that it?

GEORGE. We had our moment… for a time… at least we had that… No point wishing on… And don't you regret a single second… I know I don't…

> *A moment of intense connection between them*.

> Take care of yourself.

> GEORGE *goes*.

> *Sounds of car engines speeding faster and faster, typing faster and faster intermingled with the distorted strains of 'After the Ball is Over'*.

POPPY. Spirit of bloody Ecstasy!

> *A cacophony builds*.

> I'll give you 'Marry me!' I'll give you better half!

> *She grabs the pair of tailor's shears*.

> I'll give you fast and free!

> *She raises the shears and heads towards* SMITH*'s curtain*.

> SMITH *appears*.

SMITH. What are you doing?

POPPY. If you hadn't cut the cloth… If you hadn't stitched it up…!

SMITH. What exactly are you doing?

POPPY. I'm going to cut…

SMITH. Cut what…?

POPPY.…whatever you've been making… cut it to shreds!

SMITH. You're going to cut whatever I may have been making to shreds…?

POPPY. To stop all your fabrication… and pretence causing any more upset!

SMITH. Such a thing was never my intention…

POPPY. Why didn't you save me…?

SMITH.…from what… your own longing?

POPPY. Who can I trust now?

SMITH. There's only one person you ever need to trust…

POPPY. Oh, how could I fall for… Why did I fall…? Such a fool… Stupid stupid… And still stupid… still wanting to run as fast as my legs can carry me after him… her… Stupid!… wanting just as much to run twice as fast in the opposite direction!

She suddenly hands SMITH *the shears.*

Cut me in two… so one half can find him and never let him go… his way, all the way… wherever it takes me… I don't care…

SMITH. And the other half of you?

POPPY.…Just… please… set me… free!

SMITH. Only half of you wants to be free?

POPPY. All of me does! But what use is it… freedom… what does it matter… if if if you're all on your own.

POPPY *slumps onto the floor, giving up.*

SMITH. You know… I started to sketch… to shape… to work… with such fire… such hope… such a sense of possibility… But… peh… nothing hung right… even though it almost did… even though it promised to… nothing quite measured up… Agh… and such fine cloth!

POPPY. I tried… I really did try…

SMITH. Sometimes you've done all you can.

POPPY. Why wasn't it enough?… There must be… some other way…

SMITH. Why keep trying and trying and trying…?

POPPY. If only George wasn't…

SMITH. If George wasn't…?

POPPY. George.

SMITH. And you?

POPPY. If only I weren't…

SMITH. If you weren't…?

POPPY. If I weren't… me.

SMITH. But you are.

POPPY. How can it all lead nowhere?

SMITH. *In ergets nit…* Ah, that moment when you reach the impossible place… when you realise that… it simply doesn't hold… the dream and the substance… are never going to match. There you have it… And out come the shears… All that work… All that material… All the care…

He snips the shears.

POPPY. Such a waste.

SMITH. And once the cloth is cut, there's no putting it back into one whole piece.

POPPY. If only I'd seen in the first place.

SMITH. What did you expect?

POPPY. What anyone would expect…

SMITH. Precisely… you saw what you expected and you expected what you saw… and then it turned out that what you expected to expect wasn't what you expected…

POPPY. What was I meant to expect?

SMITH. If you hadn't expected anything then maybe you would have seen what was right in front of your nose.

POPPY. How does anyone see anything for what it is?

SMITH. Open your eyes.

POPPY. Is that all?

SMITH. Look... Really look... as if you've never seen anything ever before, because, you know what... You never know.

POPPY. Were you born knowing this?

SMITH. If I was, believe me, I keep forgetting... until it comes, the rude reminder, to shake me out of my daydreams. Why don't you take a look behind the curtain?

POPPY. What's there?

SMITH. Go on.

POPPY *goes behind the curtain.*

POPPY. Oh.

SMITH. Yes?

POPPY (*off*). It's not...

SMITH. ...what you were expecting?

POPPY (*off*). How do you...?

SMITH. Try it on.

SMITH *gets his hat, coat and a small suitcase.*

Not what I was expecting either. But then that seems to be what happens when we realise that we're making it up as we go along... isn't it?

POPPY (*off*). What on earth is this...?

SMITH. It's called a 'separable fastener'... from military uniforms... easier than buttons... Pull and it slides... zippety zip... See?

POPPY (*off*). Ah… Oh… You mean… Is it meant to be like this…?

POPPY *emerges from behind the curtain.*

She is half-dressed, wearing and adjusting a pair of flowing silk pants in dark green – ahead of their time, in a style that will become fashionable in the 1930s – a black camisole inlaid with many little black beads.

She holds a red-velvet jacket, lined with red silk.

SMITH. How does it feel?

POPPY. Different.

SMITH. Created for you, only you.

POPPY. Like a second skin…

SMITH. *Oytentish*, huh?

POPPY. Like my… birthday suit.

SMITH. Zhen Zhen De.

POPPY *touches her black-beaded camisole.*

POPPY. Did you sew all these little black beads on yourself?

SMITH. By daylight, by gaslight.

POPPY *notices* SMITH's *coat, hat and case.*

POPPY. Where are you going?

SMITH. Away now.

POPPY. Anywhere in particular.

SMITH. Probably Paris.

POPPY. Why there?

SMITH. For what else…?

POPPY.…a lady?

SMITH. She calls herself Coco. And she's making her mark. New patterns galore.

POPPY. What'll happen to me?

SMITH. Stay here as long as you like.

POPPY. Hidden away... all on my own?

SMITH. Don't you like it here?

POPPY. Oh I do... having this to come back to... down the
   alleyways and passages... through that doorway that you
   could so easily miss... leaving the hustle and bustle
   behind... To be able to escape... and be tucked away... with
   all the... wonders... the possibilities... here... But I'm not
   sure I could stay... or would even want to... without the
   ones that breathe life into everything... without the very
   person... Smith... without you... and all you've... all you...

   SMITH *takes her hand and they hold each other, hand and
   gaze, for a real moment.*

   No I don't think I can stay here anyhow... because I can't let
   myself be left behind, can I?

SMITH. It's up to you.

POPPY. Looks like I am going to have to step up and step out...
   Forwards.

SMITH. As you wish.

POPPY. I know I can get by...

SMITH. Of course...

POPPY....doing jobs like sewing, running errands, typing
   letters...

SMITH. And...?

POPPY. Maybe one day I'll even make some kind of living...
   not sure how... I mean is there ever a wage for speaking
   out... or taking action... for going against the grain?... You
   just have to give of yourself... if things are to be set right...
   And I always will, gladly.

SMITH. And...?

POPPY. Oh, there's so much more too... isn't there... that
  calls... like... it's stirring up... I don't know how to tell you
  or even tell myself... I mean, how do you follow... how can
  you trust this... whatever's in here... tucked away...
  down... in my own... deep down in here... my cares...
  beliefs... my dreams... even my mistakes... and... and...
  my... love... how can I keep all of it stored safely away any
  more?... Why would I even want to?... you know, like your
  precious red silks and velvets rolled up neatly on the
  shelves... or your sketches stashed away in hidey-holes...
  when it could be set free... to... to dance... to fly... even
  become something you can touch and hold and... and
  share... And so much that matters... all the wonders... in
  here... so many hidden wonders... they're what's calling to
  come together somehow... to find shape... their own form...
  Yes to come out... and show themselves... and be seen and
  heard and... loved... really truly loved... for who they are.

  POPPY *puts on the red jacket*.

SMITH. *Shleymesdik*.

POPPY. Bless you.

SMITH. Thank you... Thank you.

POPPY. It's all very well, but how do I dare step out looking
  like this? What would people think? Where on earth would I
  fit in?

SMITH. *Gezegenung. Zai Jian Le*. Good luck.

  SMITH *bows and goes*.

  POPPY*'s music starts to play*.

  Voices echo.

VOICES (*sing*).
  Of all that stirs in verdant field...
  Of all from fertile soil that springs...

  POPPY *pulls herself up tall*.

POPPY. Right... Oh hell...

VOICES (*sing*).
Of all the blooms that sunshine brings...

POPPY. How about... How about...?

VOICES (*sing*).
Of all that summer offers brightly...
Of all that flowers daily... nightly...

POPPY. My name is Poppy.

POPPY *holds out her hand.*

What's yours?

End.

Glossary

Zhongshan suit: tunic with straight jacket and close-fitting, stand-up collar, along with loose trousers.

Der ergster sholem… iz beser vi di beste milkhome: The worst peace is better than the best war.

Bing dong san chi… (fei yi ri zhi han): Three feet of ice does not form in a single day (as in 'Rome wasn't built in a single day' – be patient.)

Nit dos iz sheyn, vos iz sheyn, nor dos, vos es gefelt: Beautiful is not what is beautiful… beautiful is what you like.

Shleymesdik: Perfect.

Mishegas: Craziness, nonsense.

Luftmensch: airhead, impractical person with no definite business or income.

Wan shi kai tou nan: All things are difficult before they are easy.

Chutzpah: Nerve, cheek, daring.

In ergets nit: Nowhere.

Oytentish: Authentic.

Zhen Zhen de: Really real.

Gezegenung: Farewell.

Zai Jian Le: Farewell.

Other Titles in this Series

Howard Brenton
55 DAYS
#AIWW: THE ARREST OF AI WEIWEI
ANNE BOLEYN
BERLIN BERTIE
DANCES OF DEATH *after* Strindberg
DRAWING THE LINE
FAUST – PARTS ONE & TWO
    after Goethe
IN EXTREMIS
NEVER SO GOOD
PAUL
THE RAGGED TROUSERED
    PHILANTHROPISTS *after* Tressell

Jez Butterworth
JERUSALEM
JEZ BUTTERWORTH PLAYS: ONE
MOJO
THE NIGHT HERON
PARLOUR SONG
THE RIVER
THE WINTERLING

Caryl Churchill
BLUE HEART
CHURCHILL PLAYS: THREE
CHURCHILL PLAYS: FOUR
CHURCHILL: SHORTS
CLOUD NINE
DING DONG THE WICKED
A DREAM PLAY *after* Strindberg
DRUNK ENOUGH TO SAY
    I LOVE YOU?
ESCAPED ALONE
FAR AWAY
HERE WE GO
HOTEL
ICECREAM
LIGHT SHINING IN
    BUCKINGHAMSHIRE
LOVE AND INFORMATION
MAD FOREST
A NUMBER
SEVEN JEWISH CHILDREN
THE SKRIKER
THIS IS A CHAIR
THYESTES *after* Seneca
TRAPS

Helen Edmundson
ANNA KARENINA *after* Tolstoy
THE CLEARING
CORAM BOY *after* Gavin
GONE TO EARTH *after* Webb
THE HERESY OF LOVE
LIFE IS A DREAM *after* Calderón
MARY SHELLEY
THE MILL ON THE FLOSS *after* Eliot
MOTHER TERESA IS DEAD
QUEEN ANNE
SWALLOWS AND AMAZONS
    after Ransome
WAR AND PEACE *after* Tolstoy

Ian Kelly
MR FOOTE'S OTHER LEG

Liz Lochhead
BLOOD AND ICE
DRACULA *after* Stoker
EDUCATING AGNES ('The School
    for Wives') *after* Molière
GOOD THINGS
LIZ LOCHHEAD: FIVE PLAYS
MARY QUEEN OF SCOTS GOT
    HER HEAD CHOPPED OFF
MEDEA *after* Euripides
MISERYGUTS ('The Miser')
    & TARTUFFE *after* Molière
PERFECT DAYS
THEBANS *after* Euripides & Sophocles

Conor McPherson
DUBLIN CAROL
McPHERSON PLAYS: ONE
McPHERSON PLAYS: TWO
McPHERSON PLAYS: THREE
THE NIGHT ALIVE
PORT AUTHORITY
THE SEAFARER
SHINING CITY
THE VEIL
THE WEIR

Rona Munro
THE ASTRONAUT'S CHAIR
THE HOUSE OF BERNARDA ALBA
    after Lorca
THE INDIAN BOY
IRON
THE JAMES PLAYS
THE LAST WITCH
LITTLE EAGLES
LONG TIME DEAD
THE MAIDEN STONE
MARY BARTON *after* Gaskell
PANDAS
STRAWBERRIES IN JANUARY
    from de la Chenelière
YOUR TURN TO CLEAN THE STAIR
    & FUGUE

Diane Samuels
3 SISTERS ON HOPE STREET
    with Tracy-Ann Oberman
KINDERTRANSPORT
THE TRUE-LIFE FICTION OF
    MATA HARI

Jessica Swale
BLUE STOCKINGS
NELL GWYNN

Amanda Whittington
BE MY BABY
KISS ME QUICKSTEP
LADIES' DAY
LADIES DOWN UNDER
SATIN 'N' STEEL
THE THRILL OF LOVE

Tom Wells
JUMPERS FOR GOALPOSTS
THE KITCHEN SINK
ME, AS A PENGUIN

A Nick Hern Book

Poppy + George first published in Great Britain in 2016 as a paperback original by Nick Hern Books Limited, The Glasshouse, 49a Goldhawk Road, London W12 8QP, in association with Watford Palace Theatre

Poppy + George copyright © 2016 Diane Samuels

Diane Samuels has asserted her moral right to be identified as the author of this work

Cover design by Josie Richardson Photography

Designed and typeset by Nick Hern Books, London
Printed in Great Britain by CPI Books (UK) Ltd

A CIP catalogue record for this book is available from the British Library

ISBN 978 1 84842 545 3

www.nickhernbooks.co.uk

facebook.com/nickhernbooks

twitter.com/nickhernbooks